For our dear friends
Vivian and Ralph Monger
For whom my family and I are truly grateful

The Old Testament Prophets Then and Now

James M. Efird

Judson Press ® Valley Forge

Library of Congress Cataloging in Publication Data

Efird, James M.
   The Old Testament prophets then and now.

   Bibliography: p.
   1. Prophets. I. Title.
   BS1198.E33   224'.06   81-20850
   ISBN 0-8170-0960-4   AACR2

Contents

Preface 7

Chapters

  1 Introduction 9

  2 The Preexilic Prophets 33

    Elijah and Elisha 34

    Amos 36

    Hosea 44

    Isaiah 1-39 50

    Micah 61

    Zephaniah 65

    Nahum 67

    Habakkuk 69

    Jeremiah 71

    Ezekiel 78

    Isaiah 40-55 86

  3 The Postexilic Prophets 95

    Haggai 96

    Zechariah 1-8 100

    Isaiah 56-66 103

    Obadiah 107

    Jonah 108

    Malachi 111

    Joel 114

    Zechariah 9-14 117

  4 Conclusion 119

For Further Study 123

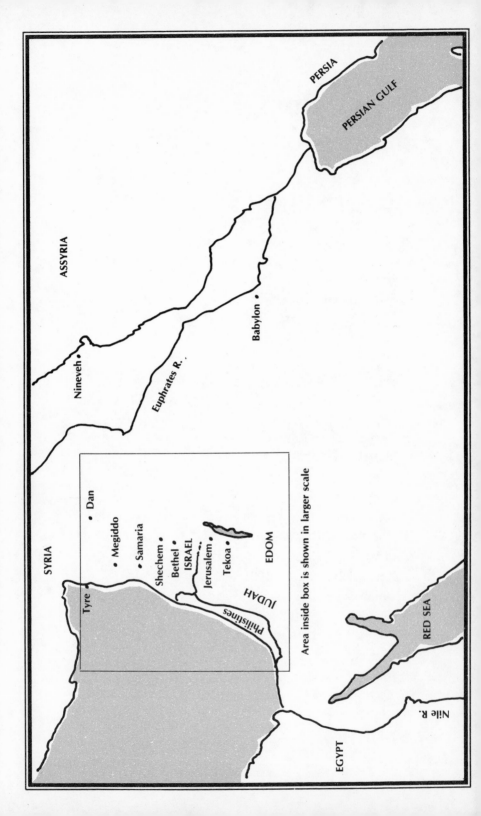

Preface

Of all the different types of biblical literature the two which are most misunderstood and abused are those works known as apocalyptic (Daniel and Revelation) and the prophetic literature. In a previous book I attempted to introduce the uninitiated lay person to apocalyptic literature (*Daniel and Revelation: A Guide to Two Extraordinary Visions*, Judson Press, 1978). The very positive response to that volume suggested that a book introducing the prophetic literature to laity might also be helpful. The present volume, then, is an attempt to explain the complexities, both historical and literary, of the prophetic books for persons who have had no formal training in biblical studies. It is designed for use by individuals and/or groups.

This book begins with an explanation of certain matters which must be understood before one attempts to interpret the prophetic writings. Secondly, there is a brief sketch of the historical period in which the prophetic movement began and ended; no biblical book can be fully understood apart from the historical context in which it originated. The bulk of the book, however, is concentrated in the examination of each prophetic book or, at points, portions of books. In these discussions there is a definite order to the presentation of the material. First, I give a brief overview of the historical background and problems relating to the prophet and the book. Secondly, I provide a short outline of the material to be studied. Because of the limitations of space, quotations from the biblical materials have been kept to a minimum; therefore you are urged to read the prophetic material carefully, keeping in mind what has been discussed and using the outline as a guide. After reading the biblical text, read the remainder of my discussion. Following that, I highly recommend a rereading of the biblical material. This study guide is only a suggestion, but I believe you will find it helpful if you follow it carefully. The purpose, of course, is to understand the biblical revelation as precisely and deeply as possible.

You will find at the conclusion of the discussion of each prophetic collection some suggestions and/or questions which should stimulate thinking as to how these great teachings may be applied to our world and our society. If you study the material with others in a group, the discussion may become quite lively!

The prophets were a major segment of the religious development of the Hebrew people as reflected in the writings of the Old Testament. Their insights, their sensitivities, and their close relationship with God make the study of them and their teachings one of the most fascinating and enjoyable of any of the biblical literature. It is my hope that something of the prophetic fire and commitment may be rekindled by those who study these faithful men of God.

I must express my deep appreciation to Mr. Harold L. Twiss, General Manager of Judson Press, for his willingness to work together with me on this project, and to the other fine people associated with Judson Press who have had a part in bringing this book to completion. My association with these people has always been a joy. I owe also a great debt to many persons too numerous to name for encouragment and support in this and other projects. Most of all I want to thank my wife, Vivian, for typing the manuscript in both rough and final form and for her constant encouragement, without which this book would not have been completed.

July, 1981   James M. Efird

CHAPTER 1

Introduction

The great proclaimers of the word of God to the people of Israel and Judah were known in the development of Israelite religion as prophets. The majority of the Old Testament is composed of collections of the sayings of these great personages and of books (Deuteronomy, Joshua, Judges, First and Second Samuel, First and Second Kings) which were greatly influenced by their basic message and teachings. The teachings of this movement have been misunderstood by differing people and groups through the centuries, even to this day. Many attempt to find in the prophetic material support for pet theories, ideas, and programs. Perhaps no other biblical literature, with the exception of the books of Daniel and Revelation, has been misunderstood and misused so extensively.

CLEARING UP SOME MISUNDERSTANDINGS

Before turning to the prophetic books *per se*, the student who is attempting to study the teachings of these majestic figures of the past must know something about the background out of which these messengers arose and the culture to which they spoke. One must also set aside some of the more popular but erroneous ideas which are currently held with relation to these men of God if their messages are to be understood.

What Is a Prophet?

One of the first misunderstandings which must be set aside is that of viewing the prophets as primarily predictors of the future. The word used for "prophet" in the Hebrew text of the Old Testament is *nabi'*, which appears to have come from an older root word *nabu*, which meant "to call." The question is whether the idea of a prophet was that of someone who "called out" (delivered a message) or someone who "was called" (selected by God to deliver a message). Perhaps both ideas were intended and understood by their supporters. Further, the Greek word for "prophet" (from which we derive our English "prophet") indicated "someone who spoke for" another. One can ascertain almost immediately, then, that foretelling the future was not a primary consideration in the total program which the prophet was compelled to undertake. Being called and delivering God's message were the two fundamental ingredients in being a prophet.

The Method of Revelation

Another area of concern and debate in dealing with the prophetic movement revolves around the question of how these extraordinary people received their revelations. In older scholarly circles it was held that the revelations were received in a state of "ecstasy." It is known that in the ancient world one sure sign of the presence of the god or a god's spirit within a person was a state of ecstatic trance, which produced wild, frenzied behavior or even catalepsy. One of the more well-known stories of the ancient world (the story of Wen-Amon) dates from about 1100 B.C. and tells of such an incident, when the spirit of the god took control of a young lad. When the boy recovered, he delivered the message of the god to the persons concerned.

It is clear that early in the prophetic movement in Israel some sort of ecstatic experiences must have formed a part of and been connected with that movement. One reads of roving ecstatic bands (1 Samuel 10:10-13; 19:20-21), of self-induced trances (2 Kings 3:15; Samuel 23-24), and of unusual experiences (1 Kings 18:46; Isaiah 6:1-7; Ezekiel 1; to name only a few), indicating that ecstatic states were part of the prophetic revelatory process. Interpreters still argue over the exact degree to which ecstasy was involved in the lives of the "major" prophets, but it is almost certain that these people were extremely intense individuals who had unique ecstatic experiences. Usually such experiences were connected with the moment of the prophetic "call," but there may have been other occasions when such episodes played a part in the prophets'understandings of God's ways.

Not all of the prophetic "visions and auditions" necessarily need be attributed to states of ecstasy, however. Quite frequently such statements as "The LORD said to me" or "The LORD showed me" can be understood as figures of speech or as the prophets' own reflections on common everyday scenes. For example, in the series of visions in Amos 7–9 most of the episodes can be understood as Amos's reflections upon events which occur in life. The prophets drew parallels between everyday scenes and Yahweh's dealing with the people and were quite fond of "plays on words" from which they received God's message. In Amos 8:1-2 it is recorded that the prophet saw an ordinary basket of "summer fruit." This word in Hebrew is *qyts*—the Hebrew is written with only consonants, the vowels being understood. In the account Yahweh asked Amos what he saw and when Amos answered "summer fruit" (pronounced *qayits* but spelled *qyts*) Yahweh began to talk about the end (pronounced *qĕts* but also spelled *qyts*) which was soon to come upon Israel. Perhaps calling such a revelation a "vision" is misleading because of modern understandings of visions. But persons wishing to understand movements from other times must learn how persons in *those* times understood certain ideas. The variety of the means of prophetic revelation is quite broad, as will be seen, but the important element for those who preserved the prophetic teachings, as well as for persons today, lies in the *meaning* of the message, not in the manner by which that message was received.

Development of the Prophetic Movement

Another closely related problem lies in the attempt to determine exactly how the prophetic movement began and how it developed up to the time when the prophets appeared with such impact within the history of Israel. Older scholarship usually saw three stages of development. There was, first of all, the *seer* stage where the prophet or holy man was consulted on matters of some urgency and importance to a person or, more commonly, a nation or people. In these instances the holy man could resort to a wide range of devices to ascertain the answer to the question presented. Sometimes animals were sacrificed and their entrails examined; on certain occasions "lots" were cast (similar to throwing of dice, drawing names from hats, or spinning pointers!). In some instances the seer was simply believed to be clairvoyant.

That stage was then followed by a period when the prophets gathered together into *roving ecstatic bands*, sometimes called (perhaps erroneously) "sons of the prophets." Their ecstatic state was believed to indicate that the spirit of the god had indeed fallen upon and taken hold of the persons so as to insure that the message ultimately delivered was genuinely the word of the god. These groups were frequently thought to have evolved into "court" prophets, i.e., in the service of the king. These prophets usually relayed the message they thought the ruler wished to hear. From this stage gradually emerged the *solitary prophet* who stood alone and delivered the message which was understood to have come from God. At one period this three-stage development theory was very popular among scholars who studied prophetic writings.

More recently, however, it has been argued that, rather than through a neatly ordered three-stage progression, the prophetic movement emerged from a coalition of two different prophetic concepts linked basically to two types of people. The advocates of this theory suggest that nomadic peoples had holy persons basically like the "seer" type, while settled agricultural peoples had those who were "ecstatic." The theory is that the Hebrew people, being originally nomadic, came into the land of Canaan in which prophets were ecstatic, and that these two religious offices gradually blended together and emerged as the "prophet" known to students of the Bible.

Such neat schemes are helpful in attempting to understand something about the background and development of the prophetic movement within Israel, but close examination of the evidence points in the direction of a much more complicated background and development. There is definite evidence that the "seer" played a part in the early stages of the prophetic movement. In 1 Samuel 9:9 one reads as a parenthetical remark in the narrative, "(. . . for he who is now called a prophet [*nabi'*] was formerly called a seer [*ro'eh*])." There is evidence also in the biblical texts of the roving ecstatic band (1 Samuel 10:10-13; 19:20-22).

There are, however, a number of other elements which seem to have formed a part of the background of the prophetic movement in its final stage. For example, one reads of groups of prophets serving in the court of the king (1 Kings 22) and of single prophets serving as court advisers (2 Samuel 7; 12:24; 1 Kings 1). It is also clear that in certain instances there was an amicable relationship between the priests and the prophets, contrary to the belief of some older interpreters that the true prophets and the priests were natural enemies. In fact, it is possible that certain prophets (such as Isaiah) may also have been priests!

Other influences which can be detected in the prophetic teachings are the style. and teaching techniques of the "wisdom" movement. "Wisdom" is a part of almost every culture; it usually begins as a commonsense approach to everyday life but gradually deals with much broader and deeper issues such as theodicy (the justice or fairness of God—why do good people suffer and evil people prosper?). "Wise men" taught by proverbs, short pithy sayings, and parables; they also used hyperbole (teaching by exaggeration) and, quite frequently, used "numerical" poetic structures (e.g., "There are three things . . . yea, four. . . ." [Proverbs 30:15, KJV]). Many of these motifs may be found incorporated within the prophetic teachings. Some influence from this quarter must have been present as the prophetic movement developed.

The picture which one derives from an examination of the data, therefore, is that of a movement with many different elements which merged together at that particular time and place to play a significant role in the development of Israelite religion. The prophetic movement appears, also, to have been directly associated with certain specific historical developments of the Israelite people. These are the development of the monarchy or kingship (beginning with Saul and David) and especially the establishment of the united kingdom under David and Solomon.

After the kingdom separated into northern Israel and southern Judah (ca. 921 B.C.), the prophetic elements continued to develop and prophetic influence became more and more prominent. During the period of the kingdoms (ca. 875–586 B.C.) this movement was at its peak. Though the movement continued into the postexilic period, the fire and vigor of the older personalities were no longer expressed by the men who prophesied after the exile. Once one realizes, however, that these religious developments were directly linked to the historical contingencies of the Hebrew people, this "decline" should not be a matter of concern. The specific circumstances in the postexilic Jewish community demanded new and different approaches to the need of the community. The prophetic style and message were simply not appropriate for that moment of history—but such matters will be discussed more fully at the appropriate points.

THE HISTORICAL SETTING

Since the historical setting is important for understanding the development of the prophetic movement, it is essential that any study of the prophets be prefaced by an examination of the historical situation which helped to produce them.

The "misty recesses of the past" of the Hebrew people reveal a conglomeration of different traditions from numerous peoples, tribes, cultures, etc., which gradually came together with David. These traditions were later blended (not always smoothly) into a single line of development upon which the nation could look as its unified past. The exact specifics of these traditions and how they were blended together do not need to be rehearsed for the purposes of this study. However, anyone studying this movement should be aware of the historical development in Israel from the time of Saul (ca. 1020 B.C.) until after the return from exile (ca. 538 B.C.).

The Need for a King

After the Hebrew people had entered the land of Canaan and settled there, they seem to have been organized into a loosely knit confederation of tribes or groups held together by a common allegiance to their God, Yahweh. Periodically certain of the groups were harassed or attacked by neighboring nations or peoples. In such instances the other tribes were supposed to come to the assistance of the one in need. Unfortunately, this did not always happen (Judges 5)! The people managed to survive, however, as separate units until a new force arrived on the scene and threatened their very existence. This danger came with the appearance of the Philistines, a group of people who had come down the coast of Palestine, fought against the Egyptians, been driven back but not really defeated, and settled on the coastland of southern Palestine. These were warlike people who were quite advanced, having iron implements and weapons of war. After settling in the area, they posed a real threat to the existence of the Hebrew tribes and kept them in a subordinate position. For example, they refused to allow the Hebrew people to have or make iron implements like theirs.

It had become increasingly clear to some of the Hebrew leaders that something else was needed to assure their existence and survival. But what could be done? The answer was fairly obvious: they needed to create a strong central government with a leader (a king in that day) who would have authority to command all the combined forces of the tribes. To some others, however, such an action was unthinkable, for to have any king other than Yahweh was an act of idolatry, an admission of lack of trust in the power of their God. This difference of opinion is clearly evident when one examines certain parts of the early history (i.e., Judges and Samuel) in which traditions favoring both sides of the argument are included. For example, there are two different traditions concerning the selection of Saul as the first "king." One depicts the event as a grudging concession by Yahweh accompanied by a warning that the people would ultimately regret their action (1 Samuel 8; 10:17-27). The other account is much more positive toward Saul and the establishment of the kingship (1 Samuel 9:1–10:16; 11; 13; 14).

Saul became the first king, ruling primarily over the northern tribes. He attempted to be a good Yahwist, outlawing such practices as magic and divination, but he came into conflict with Samuel over several matters (offering a sacrifice without authority, failing to destroy all the Amalekites) thus causing Samuel to anoint David as successor to the throne instead of Saul's heirs. After that Saul pursued David with the intention of killing him, although Saul was never successful in his attempt. David obviously felt the pressure of Saul's search, for he fled the country, becoming the leader of a motley band of questionable characters who hired themselves out as mercenaries, even fighting in the employ of the Philistines.

Growth and Split of the United Kingdom

Saul and most of his family, however, were killed fighting against the Philistines (the Philistines had sent David back to Judah for this battle!). Then David was proclaimed king in Judah with his capital at Hebron (ca. 1000 B.C.). As the result of a series of fortuitous events,[1] David's claim to the throne was unchallenged. At that point the elders of the northern tribes came to David and asked if he would rule over them also. He accepted their "gracious" request and around 994 B.C. became king over the United Kingdom.

One of David's first moves was politically brilliant. He captured the old Jebusite fortress of Jerusalem (in the south but close to the northern territory) and made it the new political and religious center of the kingdom. The ark (basically a northern religious cultic item) was brought to Jerusalem with great ceremony, and plans for a new central shrine were formulated, even though it was left to David's son Solomon actually to build the temple.

While both David and Solomon increased the territory of the kingdom and the nation experienced a time of relative prosperity, the seeds of disintegration were already at work. Even while David was king there were at least two attempts at a coup; there was much intrigue as to who David's successor would be before Solomon ultimately took the throne (2 Samuel 9–20, 1 Kings 1–2). Solomon's building projects, grandiose and famous as they were, necessitated a new program of taxation, conscription, and forced labor, which he imposed on the people by redividing the land into twelve districts not congruent with the old tribal boundaries. Since most of the people and the wealth were in the north, the heavy hand of Solomon fell hardest on these people.

---

[1] Among the most important were: the slaying of Abner, leader of the northern armies, by Joab, leader of David's army, with David disclaiming any responsibility for the deed; the murder of the last son of Saul by persons who wrongly thought that David would reward them for this deed; David's insistence on adding Saul's daughter, David's former wife, to his harem though she had remarried someone else and did not really wish to return to David.

When Solomon died, his son Rehoboam succeeded to the throne. The northern elders met him at Shechem in the north to reaffirm the covenant of kingship with the line of David. They brought with them, however, a grievance list through which they sought some relief from the oppressive practices of Solomon. Rehoboam received different advice from his two sets of advisers: one group urged him to give attention to these grievances; the other urged him not to yield and to warn the people of the north that he would be even more harsh than Solomon had been. He chose the latter advice. With that, the people of the north, led by a man named Jereboam, "seceded from the union."

Moving swiftly, Jereboam consolidated his power in the north, establishing the capital at the old Israelite shrine at Shechem and establishing two major religious centers at Dan (in the extreme north) and Bethel (in the southern part of the northern territory). At this moment the Egyptian pharaoh Shishak (or Sheshonq) invaded Palestine, causing Rehoboam to focus his attention on his defenses in Judah rather than on forcing the northern tribes back into the kingdom. By the time the Egyptians had returned to Egypt, the Northern Kingdom (now known as Israel) had become so well established that the Southern Kingdom (now known as Judah) was forced to acknowledge that any attempt to reunite the two entities was futile. This split occurred about 922 B.C.

The Northern Kingdom: Israel

It is simpler at this point to trace the history of the divided kingdoms separately rather than to attempt a simultaneous description of their development. Since the Northern Kingdom was larger, richer, and more involved in "world" politics, it is natural to examine Israel's history first. Its first king was Jeroboam I, who ruled until 901 B.C. After his death numerous internal problems arose connected with the succession to the throne. Several different persons attempted to rule, but none was able to consolidate power and establish a real dynasty.

At this point a gifted leader of the army, Omri, took control and restored stability to the land. The biblical writers give him little space, for they considered him to be evil. Politically speaking, however, he was one of the most able leaders to rule over

Israel (876–869 B.C.). He established Israel as a strong state, and foreign nations were greatly impressed with his leadership; even after his death there is reference to rulers of Israel as belonging to the house of Omri. He moved the capital to a site not recently occupied and built a new city, Samaria. It remained the seat of government for Israel until its fall in 722–721 B.C.

Because of the resurgence of the nation of Assyria to the northeast, Omri tried to establish good relations with the smaller surrounding states. Such friendship, it was thought, might be able to stem the march of the Assyrian armies into Palestine. Upon the death of Omri his more well-known son, Ahab (869–850 B.C.), ruled over Israel. His major political problems were Assyria and his immediate northern neighbor, Syria. Syria and Israel were allies in 853 B.C., however, when they joined forces to stem the march of the Assyrians at a famous battle, the battle of Qarqar. After this encounter the Assyrians did not move toward these nations for some time. This allowed Syria and Israel to begin fighting among themselves again, and in one of the battles Ahab was slain. Two of his sons followed him to the throne in quick succession.

During the reigns of Omri and Ahab in Israel there had been a new emphasis upon the worship of Baal. Ahab's wife, Jezebel, had been especially zealous in championing the worship of this god, even persecuting the prophets of Yahweh during this period. Elisha, a prophet of Yahweh and successor to Elijah, anointed Jehu, a general in the army, to be king and to lead a military coup. The house of Omri was overthrown, and the whole affair turned into a holy war bloodbath with the extermination of all the worshipers of Baal who could be found (2 Kings 10:18-27). These events took place around 842 B.C.

Because of Jehu's extensive policy of extermination most of the more capable and experienced leaders were removed, and many of the treaties established with surrounding nations were broken. Israel struggled through some very lean and trying years, being dominated by Syria to the north. But in 802 B.C. Assyria again made movements toward Palestine and defeated the Syrians. Before Assyria could conquer Israel, other problems within the empire caused the Assyrians to leave. This allowed Israel to expand her own boundaries, and a period of growth and prosperity emerged. It was during this period that the first of the "classical" prophets appeared. The king during this period was Jereboam II (786–746 B.C.).

In 747 B.C. a new king, Tiglath-pileser III, had taken control of Assyria, and he inaugurated a renewed policy of expansion for the Assyrian empire. After the death of Jeroboam II in 746 B.C. there was a period of political confusion in Israel, with at least six rulers in the course of only a few years. Israel, and what was left of a government in Syria, desperately attempted to rally the smaller neighboring states into a coalition to fight the Assyrians. This had been successful before in the time of Ahab, but it would not be this time. The alliance was called the Syro-Ephraimitic alliance (ca. 735 B.C.), and the nations in this group attempted to force others to join. Judah was one of those who was "asked" to join but did not wish to do so. By 733 B.C. the alliance was crushed by Assyria. The last king of Israel, Hoshea, ruled over only a portion of what had formerly been the nation Israel; the remainder had been incorporated into the Assyrian Empire.

Not knowing when he was well off, Hoshea revolted in 727 B.C., the year that Tiglath-pileser III died. This was a fatal mistake. The new Assyrian king, Shalmaneser V, entered the area and laid seige to Samaria. His death occurred before the siege was completed, but his successor, Sargon II, completed the job (722–721 B.C.). The northern Israelites were deported to other lands, scattered among strange peoples, and finally blended into these other cultures. The few people left in the land were poorer and less educated, and when Assyria imported peoples from other places to populate the area, these Israelites merged with the new peoples to form another culture. The people of southern Judah regarded these people as "impure" and "unclean."

The Southern Kingdom: Judah

On returning to examine the fortunes of the southern kingdom of Judah, one must keep in mind that this section of Palestine was off the beaten path and much less important economically or politically than its northern neighbor. This may have been the reason why Judah survived for a longer period of time than Israel.

During the years immediately following the split between the two areas, Israel and Judah remained at odds with each other.

When Omri came to the throne of Israel, however, he wished to make an ally of Judah rather than continue the enmity between them. He and his son, Ahab, did their best to keep good relations with Judah, even marrying the daugher of Ahab and Jezebel (Athaliah) to the son of Jehoshaphat, the Judean king. When the Jehu revolution took place in Israel, the king of Judah was killed, and Athaliah attempted to have all members of the Davidic line eradicated. She then controlled the Judean government in Jerusalem. Her infant grandson was secretly hidden in the temple by the priests, however, and was proclaimed king when he was seven years old. At this time Athaliah was slain; she had been the only non-Davidic ruler to sit on the throne of Judah prior to the Babylonian exile.

The fortunes of the two nations roughly paralleled each other. When one experienced difficult times, the other did; and when one had a period of prosperity, the other did also. Their destinies began to exhibit very different courses with the rise of Tiglath-pileser III in Assyria, however. When Assyria began to move into Palestine, Israel and Syria formed an alliance (as already noted) to contest the Assyrian menace. They tried to force Judah to join the alliance at that time (ca. 735–734 B.C.), but the Judean king, Ahaz, appealed to Tiglath-pileser III for aid. (Becoming a political ally, especially a minor one, of a larger and more powerful country not only entailed the sending of tribute, fighting for the stronger nation if called upon, etc., but it also meant acknowledging the gods of the superior state, even erecting places of worship for these gods!) Assyria was exceedingly happy to have another ally and source of money and people at its disposal. Thus when Israel was destroyed, Judah was spared.

Hezekiah became king of Judah in 715 B.C. At first Judah remained in a position of subservient alliance to Assyria, but when a new king came to the Assyrian throne in 705 B.C., Hezekiah inaugurated a religious reform. Such a move had not only moral and religious dimensions but political ramifications as well. It was, in effect, a revolt against Assyria. The new Assyrian king, Sennacherib, was not too busy to attend to this effrontery. He and his army invaded the area in about 701 B.C. and captured forty-six walled cities of Judah, and according to Assyrian accounts, "shut up" Hezekiah like "a bird in a cage" in Jerusalem. Something happened, however, which caused

Sennacherib to return to Assyria without capturing Jerusalem. He had already won many concessions from Hezekiah, even taking several of Hezekiah's daughters back to Assyria with him as his concubines. The deliverance of Jerusalem was so dramatic, however, that many people began to believe that Yahweh would never allow his city to be taken! This proved to be a very mistaken and dangerous interpretation of what had transpired.

After the death of Hezekiah, his son Manasseh became king in Judah. His reign (687/6–642 B.C.) was the longest of any of the southern kings. According to the writers of the Deuteronomic history (Judges through Kings), Manasseh was the worst king ever to reign in Judah. Almost immediately it became evident that his policy was to ally Judah with Assyria, which meant that Assyria's gods were reestablished in the land. In addition to this, many other unsavory religious practices were reenacted during Manasseh's reign: ritual prostitution, divination, magic, astral worship, even human sacrifice.

When Manasseh died, his son Amon came to the throne but was soon assassinated. After a short period of confusion the young son of Amon was proclaimed king (about 640 B.C.). His name was Josiah, and he was only eight years old! Obviously a strong priestly element in the capital supported the lad, and they trained him well. It was also a fortuitous time for him to be king. Egypt was very weak and Assyria was in the process of disintegration. Politically, then, Josiah consolidated his authority over the area, even extending the territory of Judah, especially to the north. He may even have entertained dreams of reestablishing the nation as it had existed in the times of David and Solomon.

Josiah is more famous, however, for the great religious reform inaugurated during his reign. According to the account in 2 Kings 22–23, a "book of the law" was discovered in the temple during a time when it was being cleaned and repaired. This scroll was taken and read to King Josiah, who was so moved that he made the teachings contained in it the basis for a religious reform. There is some discussion among scholars as to what that book actually was. Some think that it was the book of Deuteronomy as we now have it; others argue that it was a collection of traditions which became the basis for the later book of Deuteronomy. There are those who have surmised that the book itself was a "plant" by the religious leaders to encourage a reform movement, while others hold that the traditions included in the document were indeed old and had, in fact, been lost during the reign of Manasseh. Whatever the solutions to those questions, it is clear that the elements of the reform seem to coincide with the stipulations of Deuteronomy 12–26 and 28.

The reform, sometimes called the Josianic reform and sometimes known as the Deuteronomic reform, was aimed at a purge of all foreign religious elements. The worship of Yahweh alone was allowed. All practices of magic and divination, as well as all astral worship, were forbidden; human sacrifice was outlawed. The most important element of these changes, however, was the stipulation that all outlying shrines and holy places be closed, even those dedicated to the worship of Yahweh. *All* worship had to be celebrated in the Jerusalem temple, which would give some control over and standardize the religious practices of the people. The reform movement gave some hope to certain religious leaders that the land would prosper again after the pagan elements had been purged from the worship of Yahweh. Among the people, however, an even greater confidence began to grow based upon the escape of Jerusalem from the Assyrians at the time of Hezekiah and upon the new emphasis on Yahweh's presence in the temple in Jerusalem. Many began to think that nothing harmful could possibly happen to God's people in God's land, especially God's city!

World events, however, would soon dictate some changes in the history of Judah. At this time (ca. 626–612 B.C.) Assyria was being defeated by the rising power of Babylonia. Egypt, never a country to mind its own business in those days and fearful of a strong Babylonia, decided that it should assist its old enemy, Assyria. In 609 B.C., therefore, the Egyptian pharaoh Necho (or Neco) marched with an army through Palestine to assist Assyria in the fighting. Josiah, sympathetic if not actually allied with Babylonia, felt it his duty to fight the Egyptians and met them at Megiddo, a famous battle site in the old northern territory. His forces were defeated, and he was killed. His son, Jehoahaz, succeeded him, but the Egyptians immediately placed Jehoahaz's brother, Eliakim, on the throne to serve as a vassal of Egypt, changing his name to Jehoiakim. During Jehoiakim's reign his father's reform movement died.

Babylonia defeated the Egyptians in 605 B.C. at one of the famous battles of antiquity, the battle of Carchemish. Palestine thus came under the complete control of the Babylonians, who were relatively enlightened rulers for their time. They left Jehoiakim on the throne in Judah, but he remained strongly pro-Egyptian. Egypt constantly attempted to persuade the smaller nations in the area to rebel against Babylonia. And in 600 B.C. Judah did rebel. It proved to be a fatal mistake. The great general and king, Nebuchadnezzar, marched into the land in 598 B.C. and captured Jerusalem in 597 B.C. Before the nation fell, however, Jehoiakim died. There is some uncertainty about whether his death was by natural causes or by assassination. His son Jehoiachin came to the throne only to surrender to the Babylonians and be carried off into exile to Babylon. Many other high ranking persons were also deported. The Babylonians, however, were very lenient with Judah. They allowed the nation to continue and even placed a Davidic descendant on the throne as king. Jehoiachin's uncle Mattaniah was named king and his name changed to Zedekiah.

This man, unfortunately for the people of Judah, was a very weak ruler. He usually understood what he ought to do but was too weak to resist the powerful pro-Egyptian element still among the leadership in the land. Egypt continued to encourage the smaller states to resist Babylonian rule. One rebellion almost broke out in 594 B.C. but did not materialize. In 589 B.C. Judah revolted against Babylonia for the last time! The Babylonian army came into the land, destroyed Jerusalem and the temple, and carried off most of the people into Babylonian exile. After this took place around 586 B.C., Judah ceased to exist as a nation and became part of the district of Samaria under the Babylonian system of administration.

The Babylonians settled the "Judahite" people near the city of Babylon. There was initially an undercurrent of expectation among those people that they would soon be allowed to return, but that hope grew dim very quickly. They were allowed to live in relative peace, however, and ultimately made for themselves a comfortable existence. After the great king Nebuchadnezzar died, there was no political figure in Babylonia who was able to consolidate his gains or inspire confidence among the Babylonian people. Therefore the Babylonian empire slowly began to crumble and in 539 B.C. was conquered by the great Persian leader, Cyrus. This man was a most enlightened ruler and allowed exiles to return to their homelands and to worship their own gods. Thus, in 538 B.C. the Jewish people were allowed to return home. By now almost two generations had passed; most of the people had never known any home except Babylon, and many did not wish to leave. Some did, however, and in 538 B.C. a group returned to Judah led by a man named Sheshbazzar. Interestingly enough, after the people arrived, Sheshbazzar was heard of no more.

At this point, a Davidic descendant named Zerubbabel began to emerge as a political figure among the restored people. Judah was not an independent state, however, but rather was part of the Persian district of Samaria. Hopes obviously were running high for a restoration of the nation and a return to the former glories of David and Solomon. These hopes must have centered in Zerubbabel, who, strangely enough, suddenly disappeared from the scene. After this there seems to have been very little real political activity for some time. The community was basically organized and structured around the temple (which had been rebuilt around 515 B.C.) and the high priest, a societal structure which some call a "theocratic" (God-ruled) community.

Oddly enough there is very little known specifically about the history of the Jewish people in Judah after the return from exile. What few sources there are do not always give a coherent account of what was happening to the struggling community. What is clear is that the people were economically poor, politically powerless, and militarily helpless to protect themselves from surrounding nations or from the ebb and flow of major armies which passed through the area periodically.

What is known (and some scholars argue over some of the specifics even here) is this:

—the people returned in 538 B.C. to find a desolate land and destroyed cities with the people who were already there suspicious and at times hostile toward the returnees;

—the temple was rebuilt about 520–515 B.C.;

—there may have been some sort of military action against the area ca. 485 B.C. which again destroyed the temple, but this is mainly conjectural;

—in 444 B.C. and 432 B.C. Nehemiah was allowed to return to

Judah from Persia and assisted the people in rebuilding the walls of Jerusalem, repopulating it, and establishing some guidelines to strengthen the struggling community;

—ca. 398 B.C. Ezra came from Babylon with a "book of the law" and helped to organize and to structure further the community life of the people, centering their lives around the "law";

—in 331 B.C. Alexander the Great defeated the Persians and overran that area of the world;

—upon his death in 323 B.C., wars broke out among his generals to determine who would rule over his empire;

—by 301 B.C. the wars concluded with the division of the empire into four segments, two of which were important for the people of Judah: the general Ptolemy had control over Egypt and southern Palestine and the general Seleucus had control over most of the old Persian empire and northern Palestine;

—Judah was caught in the subsequent fighting between the Ptolemies and the Seleucids for control of that area, which was finally won by the Seleucids ca. 198 B.C.

One can readily see that the people of Judah were subject to the power struggles of the major nations as well as vulnerable to the smaller, more established nations surrounding them. This meant that the community was always weak and unable to determine its own destiny. Many persons decided to leave the area during this period, journeying to other nations and establishing themselves in communities over much of the Graeco-Roman world. It was at this time that the synagogue was established as a religious as well as social center for these dispersed people.

In a sense, however, our brief survey of the historical era in which the prophetic movement flourished has overstepped its bounds, for the postexilic era (after 538 B.C.) saw the decline and demise of the classical prophets. The basic reason for this was not that God was no longer revealing himself to the community, but rather that the historical context no longer really called for the proclamation of the prophet. Other religious developments were taking place, including the emphasis on the written Law and the proper interpretation of that Law, the flowering of the wisdom movement (which produced the books of Proverbs, Job, and Ecclesiastes), and the rise and development of the apocalyptic thought patterns and literature (basically reflected in the Book of Daniel). New times and circumstances called for different modes of revelation, and God worked through these as the circumstances dictated.

The prophetic movement was such an integral part of the historical period of the monarchy and the kingdoms that one cannot really begin to understand the messages of the prophets unless one has at least some knowledge of the historical events of those times. The truth of this will be demonstrated rather specifically as the individual prophetic collections are examined.

GUIDELINES FOR STUDY OF THE PROPHETIC BOOKS

Before we turn to the specific study of the individual prophets, there are several points which should be noted and kept in mind with regard to the proper interpretation of the prophetic material.

The prophetic literature in the Bible is found in the Hebrew canon under the heading "prophets" and is divided into two sections: the Former Prophets and the Latter Prophets. This book deals with what are called the Latter Prophets, and there are basically four books or scrolls in that collection. They are Isaiah, Jeremiah, Ezekiel, and what is known as the Book of the Twelve, which contains the twelve so-called minor prophets. My discussion of the individual prophets does not follow this order but is organized chronologically.

It must be clearly understood that the prophets were primarily proclaimers, not writers. The prophets did not write down their teachings, even though there is evidence that in a few cases the prophets caused some of their teachings to be written down (Jeremiah, for example). The fact that the prophets were speakers, however, accounts for the fear and, at times, hatred with which they were viewed by the people. In that era of history the spoken word was believed to have an inner efficacy of its own: it carried within itself the power to accomplish the spoken intent. Thus, when the prophet announced doom on the nation, the people looked upon him as a traitor.

Understanding Hebrew Poetry

During the past generation scholars have concentrated on the manner in which the prophets delivered their messages. The first point to keep in mind is that the prophetic oracles were delivered primarily in poetic form. This fact by itself should alert interpreters of the prophetic message to recall that poetry in any language is not intended to be understood in the same way as narrative prose. Some understanding of Hebrew poetry is essential if one is to recognize it and interpret it correctly.

Hebrew poetry is characterized by a phenomenon known as parallelism; this is displayed in two-line couplets in which the second line relates to the first in one of several ways. There are three such types of parallelism: (1) the second line repeats the meaning of the first line in different words; (2) the second line states the opposite, or antithesis, of the first line; and (3) the second line builds upon the meaning of the first line, carrying that meaning a step further. (When reading the prophetic material, it is best to use a translation which prints the poetry as poetry, as does the RSV.)

The Form of the Message

A closely related area of interest lies in the question of precisely what form the prophet used to deliver the message. A "form" involves a specific formula or structure involving several components which lead to a specific type of saying. Many scholars believe that the "messenger" form was the primary one used in the prophetic teachings. The messenger form evolved from a setting in which a person in authority would send a trusted servant to deliver a message to another person or group. It was understood that the messenger spoke with the same authority as the superior who had sent him. In a more precise study one would examine the explicit steps included in the form which led up to the the central message itself. Such study is known in scholarly circles as form criticism. This area of scholarship, however, is highly speculative and conjectural, and while it is of some importance in the understanding of the prophetic message, a detailed analysis of these forms is not appropriate for this study. Suffice it to say that when such elements are important to the discussion, they will be noted.

Other forms for prophetic messages were the "threat" (both individual and collective), the "reproach" (giving the reason for a judgment), exhortations, laments, "call" stories (stories detailing the "call" which the person received to become a prophet), "lawsuits," taunt songs, dialogues, hymns, and others. One can readily understand why there is little unanimity of opinion among the form-critical scholars as to precisely what the basic "form" was with regard to the prophetic teachings. What should be kept in mind is that the prophets, as inspired persons of God, were not limited to one or two forms in the announcement of their messages but utilized whatever method was appropriate for the moment. The richness and variety of their preaching were part of what made them special.

Transmission of the Message

More important perhaps than the exact "form" of the original proclamation of the prophetic teachings is some understanding of how these teachings were preserved and transmitted. Exactly how this was done can only be a conjecture, but it appears likely that the sayings were passed along orally over a long period of time. Some have argued that there were "schools" of disciples identified with each prophetic figure whose members preserved and transmitted the teachings of the great master. There is some evidence that such "schools" may have existed, but there is no concrete and irrefutable proof that they did. What appears to be more likely is that different groups within the religious communities of Israel and Judah valued, preserved, and transmitted the words of the prophets which they felt spoke most directly to the community and the needs of the people. There may have been individual "schools" for certain of the more revered and productive prophetic personalities like Isaiah, but other groups may have preserved the teachings of several prophets. As time passed some of the teachings began to be grouped together and probably written down by those passing along this material. These smaller units were later placed together to form larger units. From the various units, oral and written, the later prophetic books emerged. In most cases these groups not only preserved the teachings but also attempted when appropriate to apply them to new contexts and situations. (This is exactly what persons today attempt to do with biblical teachings.)

Later Editing

An understanding of the transmission process leads naturally into a discussion of how the prophetic books were edited into the body of literature as it now exists. Since the prophetic oracles (sayings) were delivered at different times and different places, and since these oracles were preserved and passed along orally from generation to generation, it is obvious that in the existing arrangement of the collected sayings there is going to be little or no chronological order. It is also clear from careful study that much of the material in particular books had been collected into smaller units between the time of the oral pronouncement and the final written form. Some of these units appear to have been brought together because of similar content, some by "catch-word" (in which the same word is featured prominently in each of the sayings in a group of oracles), some because of biographical interest, and some because of other rationales. This means that each of the prophetic oracles must be examined in the light of its original context (insofar as that can be ascertained) and in the light of its present context, i.e., how the final editors of the prophetic books incorporated those sayings into the final structure of the completed collection.

Since the prophetic books were edited in the postexilic period, one should not be surprised to learn that certain concerns of the postexilic community were sometimes incorporated into the preexilic prophetic teachings. (Certain of these motifs will be noted specifically as the individual books are examined.) Older scholars attempted to deal with this problem by postulating that the preexilic prophets were proclaimers of doom upon the nation, and the exilic and postexilic prophets announced hope to a chastised and burdened people. Therefore, any hopeful passage in a preexilic prophetic book was considered a postexilic insertion into the thought of the preexilic prophet. If a doom passage was found in the postexilic books, it was treated as a preexilic oracle misplaced into a postexilic setting. While it is true that the preexilic prophets were primarily proclaimers of doom and the postexilic prophets proclaimers of hope, there is no longer any attempt to separate these two emphases as rigidly as older scholarship had done. What one must do is examine each book and each teaching to determine whether a specific oracle is appropriate to the particular prophet and to the society and context within which he worked.

Further, it must be reiterated that the final editors were not simply recounting God's words as delivered by these inspired messengers to the people of the past, but they were, by the publication of these collections of teachings, also attempting to apply these lessons to their own times, problems, and lives. The task of the modern-day interpreter is no less than that!

The Ancient Mindset

In order to interpret properly the specific teachings and content of the prophetic books, one must be reminded that the ideas and thought patterns of the prophets' times were different from those of our culture. To be aware of some of their modes of thinking may help the modern interpreter better understand the message and guard against some very unlikely interpretations.

One of the most important concepts is that the ancient world generally thought in terms of corporate units rather than of individuals. The group and its survival were most crucial to these people; therefore, the emphasis in that culture and society was upon the corporate entity. Individuals were important also, but primarily as they contributed to the well-being of the group or as they were detrimental to it. Such thinking was also part of the Hebrew culture. In fact, the Hebrews developed such an understanding of this type of thinking that they believed that the group *was* the individual and the individual *was* the group. This idea was not intended as a symbolic understanding, as modern people would reason, but as an actualization of the group and individual being one and the same. For example, if an individual sinned, the group was punished. And if an individual who had sinned was found guilty, his entire family could be judged along with him (see Joshua 7 for a classic example). This type of thinking is commonly known as the concept of "corporate personality."

Understanding this idea is absolutely essential if someone wishes to interpret properly the prophetic messages (most of the Old Testament writings reflect this basic teaching). Some contemporary persons do not realize that corporate identity was so important to the people of that era; it is true that most persons today do not think in this way. The fact that such ideas are different from our thinking, however, should not hinder the modern interpreter from understanding and interpreting those concepts as the ancients believed them. One should also be alert to the truth which is inherent in their understandings. For example, human beings today *still* exist in and derive strength from groups. What nourishes or destroys a group nourishes or destroys the individual, and vice versa.

One other idea complementary to the concept of corporate thinking was the belief that all members of the group, both past and future, were in some way present within the existent group. Therefore, if the present group was being punished for sin, all members past and future were also involved in the punishment. As already indicated, such thinking seems rather strange to twentieth-century minds. Being constantly aware of the concept of "corporate personality" will greatly assist the student of the prophetic literature in understanding many passages which would seem rather nonsensical otherwise.

Another interesting area which the modern interpreter must not overlook concerns the ancient Hebrews' ideas about death. The Hebrews did not believe in life after death with rewards and punishments. Neither did they believe in annihilation. They believed that at death every person (rich, poor, king, pauper, slave, free—*all* people) went to the place of the dead—a gloomy, dark, shadowy realm in the depths of the earth called Sheol. There were no rewards or punishments in this place, only the weakest kind of existence one could imagine. Somehow, they believed, the barrenness of this place could be alleviated somewhat if there was a "link" to the land of the living through descendants. Exactly how this helped was never precisely explained.

Since all went to Sheol at death and since there were no rewards or punishments there, this world became the most important place for reward or punishment—in fact, the only place. Early in the history of Israelite religious thinking, a certain understanding of a "system" in life developed in relation to God's will and purposes. This "system" is sometimes known in Old Testament study as the "Deuteronomic" theology. The basic idea was that if one was obedient to God's laws, that person would be rewarded with a good life—prosperity, absence of problems, long life, etc. If, however, one was not obedient to God's laws, that person would be punished by experiencing problems, bad luck, illness, and the like. Such an idea was based, obviously, on the premise that if one were to be either rewarded or punished, the judgment would have to take place during one's lifetime.

In studying the prophetic teachings it is necessary for the reader to remember that the basic theological premises of the prophets were heavily influenced by these ideas related to corporate personality and the Deuteronomic theology.

Prophetic Signs

One other phenomenon, and a fascinating one at that, of which the modern interpreter should be aware when studying the prophetic literature is that of the "prophetic sign." These curious activities are primarily responsible for certain modern tendencies to think of the prophets as weird or strange. Isaiah walking around the streets of Jerusalem naked, Ezekiel lying on his side for 430 days, and Jeremiah taking the elders to a gate of the city just to watch him break a flask are illustrations of the prophetic sign.

These actions were more than simply strange behavior in the culture of that time; they were the product of belief in sympathetic or mimetic magic. Just as words were considered to contain certain power within themselves, so certain actions were believed to have inherent power which would assist in the completion of the idea being portrayed through the action. For example, if one wanted rain, one could devise some sort of ritual which would include the pouring of water as a central aspect. It was believed that the smaller act would in some way insure that the larger act would come to pass. Since the Hebrew people were part of the ancient culture which embraced these ideas, these ideas were part of their thinking also. The Hebrew prophets, however, never thought that these actions could be done arbitrarily by human beings or that such actions could bind God to do their bidding. The prophets performed these actions not at their own initiative but, they believed, at the command of God. Nevertheless, these activities were understood by them and the people as being an important element in the accomplishment of certain deeds and events within the historical process. Some of these signs will be discussed more fully when the individual prophets are studied in detail.

With these preliminary discussions in mind, one can now turn to a study of the individual prophets, their teachings, and their collected sayings.

CHAPTER 2

The Preexilic Prophets

As already indicated, there were numerous tributaries flowing into the large stream which ultimately became the classical prophetic movement in Israel. Samuel, for example, was a seer as well as a judge and kingmaker; Gad and Nathan were obviously court prophets but also served as political advisers to the kings. From the beginning, however, the political element was prominent. One finds the prophets almost always involved in the political events of the nation(s).

Early in the movement groups of prophets connected with the court of the king seem to have evolved. The purpose of such prophets was to advise the king on important matters and to offer "good words" for the success of a project (quite frequently a battle or war) and "curses" against foreign nations who were enemies of the nation. It is fairly certain that at this stage the prophets had become pawns of the king, saying what he wanted to hear. Those who disagreed feared for their lives. One good illustration of this can be seen in the story of Micaiah ben-Imlah (1 Kings 22). This account illustrates the emergence of the single, solitary figure who fearlessly proclaimed the word of Yahweh to leaders and people alike.

ELIJAH AND ELISHA

As the biblical texts present the available data, it appears that *the* beginning of the movement which produced the solitary prophets should be attributed to the person of Elijah the Tishbite. Elijah appeared on the scene in northern Israel (after the division of the kingdom of David and Solomon) during the reign of Ahab (ca. 869–850 B.C.). The strong king Omri, father of Ahab, had consolidated his power in Israel, established a new political center at Samaria, and attempted to make treaties and alliances with the surrounding nations. One such alliance was consummated by the marriage of his son Ahab to the Tyrian princess, Jezebel. This woman was a strong personality and exerted great influence over her husband; since she was a follower of the god Baal, she actively encouraged the worship of Baal in the nation of Israel. Such encouragement did not go unappreciated, for many of the people who had lived in the northern area over the centuries had been Baal worshipers. Along with this emphasis on the worship of Baal came a corresponding de-emphasis on the worship of Yahweh, perhaps even a persecution of the leaders of the Yahweh cult. In terms of religious allegiance, the nation of Israel was rapidly becoming a state where Baal was considered its chief god.

Into this situation came the lone figure of Elijah. He appeared as a desert wanderer, a person apart from the official religious orders, who was called by Yahweh to challenge the people's worship of Baal. This challenge was made at the point of Baal's strength. The people of Canaan had understood Baal to be the god of fertility, who provided rain for the crops which fed people and animals and gave life to the land. Elijah appeared in the court of Ahab and announced that it would not rain again in Israel until Yahweh commanded it. Perhaps this threat was scarcely noticed until the drought lasted into the second year. Then Ahab began a diligent search for the bearer of ill tidings. Elijah hid from Ahab, finally reappearing to challenge the prophets of Baal to a duel (1 Kings 18).

Many persons miss the real meaning of this duel because they tend to focus on the appearance of the fire. Fire quite frequently is a key element in Old Testament "theophany" accounts, stories in which God appears at a particular place at a particular time to accomplish a particular purpose (the experience of Moses in

Exodus 3, for example). But the real issue in the confrontation between Elijah and the prophets of Baal was: Who gives the rain? The stakes were high; not only was the god who lost the contest to be worshiped no longer in Israel, but the prophets of that god were to be killed! In reading the story one notes with interest the pouring out of the water by Elijah. In addition to the dramatic account of Elijah's confrontation with the prophets of Baal, there are several other delightful stories told about Elijah (and Elisha, his successor) in First and Second Kings. The most interesting feature about these stories is the fact that they portray these two prophets of Yahweh as demonstrating powers in the name of Yahweh which many people of that time felt belonged only to Baal. Thus, with the person of Elijah came the clear message—Yahweh is God in Israel.

Elijah's successor, Elisha, followed in the footsteps of his mentor, and many of the stories told about Elijah are paralleled in the Elisha traditions. Elisha, however, does not appear to have been a lone, solitary figure but is found with a group of prophets who may have looked to him for leadership (see the Elisha stories in 2 Kings 2–13). His career was dedicated to the continuation of Elijah's zeal that Israel worship only Yahweh. The stories about Elisha demonstrate that Yahweh is the one who gives life and controls nature, not Baal.

Elisha's political involvement became evident when he anointed Jehu, a general of the army, to become king over Israel. This was done while the house of Omri still governed; in short, Elisha was heavily involved in a coup to overthrow the government! In time Jehu did overthrow the Omrid dynasty in a bloody period of history which involved even the slaughter of the king of Judah. To rid the land of Baal worshipers Jehu proclaimed a great festival of celebration in honor of Baal, and all Baal devotees were invited. When they had assembled, he had the area secured and ordered his troops to kill them all (2 Kings 10:18-28). Such activity seems strange and barbaric to us, but such slaughter in a "holy war" was standard procedure for that time and place. Elisha's political influence thus cemented the religious gains for the worship of Yahweh which Elijah's ministry had begun.

The power of Baal was so deeply ingrained in the northern area, however, that even the excesses of Jehu did not completely eradicate it. Certain practices and ideas continued but were assimilated more and more into the cultic rituals of the worship of Yahweh. It is to this situation that Amos and Hosea, the first of the great prophets whose teachings were collected into specific books, spoke.

AMOS

The first of the great classical prophets spoke to the Northern Kingdom, but he was from Judah! Amos, from Tekoa, described himself as one who tended the flocks and who was a keeper of sycamores (probably a type of Near Eastern fig-bearing plant). The superscription to the book also identifies him as a shepherd. He appeared on the scene at Bethel, one of the northern shrines, during the reign of Jereboam II (ca. 750 B.C.). During this period (786–746 B.C.) both Egypt and Assyria were rather weak, and Syria had been defeated by the Assyrians earlier; consequently Israel experienced a period of political and economic prosperity. The people and their leaders believed that this was God's method of rewarding them for doing right. According to Amos's accounts, the people were flocking to the religious shrines to continue the rituals to insure God's blessings for the future.

To Amos, however, the situation looked quite different. Beneath the exterior appearance of peace and well-being, there was no real substance to the religious commitment of the people, especially those in positions of power and leadership. The business community cheated the people, and the court system was corrupt, with judgments being awarded according to the largest briber. The social structure was fast becoming divided into two segments, the rich and the poor, with the rich becoming more and more callous towards those who were less fortunate.

Amos's message in the midst of this situation was one of outrage, not because he personally was pronouncing judgment on the sins of the nation but because Yahweh, God of Israel, had run out of patience. It is of some importance to note at the outset of the study of the prophets that in the biblical accounts judgment is never imposed so that God can "get even" with those who sin; judgment is always for the purpose of redemption. Quite frequently the nation would experience certain tragedies which were viewed as "warnings" by the prophets. These may be called "partial" judgments, and the warnings were understood as sent by God for the purpose of causing the people to repent. After a period of time, however, God's patience was exhausted when it became clear that the people were not going to heed the warnings. When that point came, a "final" judgment was inevitable. Amos appeared in such a time.

If there is one major theme which best characterizes the message of Amos, it is that of righteousness (and its companion, justice). But righteousness to Amos was not simply a human ideal or set of standards; rather, righteousness was the essential nature and being of Yahweh, God of Israel. Righteousness, therefore, was rooted in God's being, and righteousness could then be required of human beings because it was the natural consequence of relating properly to God. Yahweh was righteous; he did what was right and always acted in accordance with his nature. Whatever God decreed and however God acted, then, was righteous. Thus the requirements for God's people were viewed not as humanly created but in accord with the principles which derived directly from God's own nature. Human righteousness meant abiding by the law given by God, especially as it related to rendering fair justice in the courts of law, in the business community, and in people's daily relationships with other people.

As for the final structure of the book of Amos, it appears that there are two major collections which formed the basis for the book: a collection of oracles of doom against both foreign nations and the nation of Israel (1–6) and a series of visions (7:1-9; 8:1-3; 9:1-6). These two units, which were probably put together at different times, were interspersed with other smaller units including sayings, doxologies, and oracles. Finally, the completed work was furnished with an ending which envisioned a restoration of God's people.

Study Outline for the Book of Amos

  I. Oracles Against Nations: 1:3–2:5
 II. Oracles Against Israel: 2:6–6:14
III. Visions: 7:1–9:4
       Amos and the priest at Bethel: 7:10-17
 IV. Final Words of Yahweh: 9:5-15

Oracles Against Nations

The first major section of the Book of Amos includes a collection of oracles against foreign nations. These proclamations were directed at the nations closest to Israel and with whom Israel had had encounters (many of which were bad) in the past. The basic teaching of this section appears to be that Yahweh could and would exercise judgmental authority over those nations not normally thought to be under his authority. These judgments were based upon a "fair," or just, foundation even though those nations had not acknowledged Yahweh as their God and had not received the special revelation of Yahweh as the people of Israel had. The basis for the judgment rested upon a generally held idea of that era, namely that there were certain accepted and understood codes of conduct recognized by the nations, and these codes were supposed to be morally binding upon the nations. When, therefore, nations exceeded these understood limits, Yahweh would punish them because they were not acting "rightly." Yahweh's power was not limited to Israel only!

The stylized list of oracles (the literary structure, "For three transgressions, . . . and for four . . .") described sins including extraordinary atrocities (1:3, 11, 13; 2:1), nations carrying off entire populations into exile (a grievous crime in ancient society [1:6, 9]), and Judah's breaking the law of Yahweh (2:4-5). In each of these instances the punishment was depicted as God's sending a "fire" upon the nation. Quite clearly in Amos's teaching, the term "fire" refers to a military conquest. This idea that military conquest is God's most hideous judgment was a common idea in the prophetic teachings. In all probability this idea resulted from the fact that in human history the most terrible calamity which could befall a nation was to be conquered by an enemy army. The horrors of war—famine, slaughter, atrocities, pillage, rape, and all the other gory elements—have been all too real to every generation of human history. What more graphic way to depict judgment upon evil nations? Amos believed that Yahweh was ultimately directing the course of human history to insure that his righteousness would finally prevail.

Oracles Against Israel

Having enumerated the sins of the surrounding nations, Amos (or the final editors of the book) turned to the central concern of the teaching—the enumeration of the sins of Israel. As one reads through the oracles in this section of the book (2:6–6:14), one is struck with the recurrence of several themes. First of all, and most importantly, there is the pervasive idea that the people of Israel were not "righteous." They were superifically religious, going through the motions of worship but not properly committed to God. This situation resulted in some people exploiting others, especially those who were economically and politically powerless (2:6-7a). The people also participated in unsavory religious practices (2:7-8) and were unable to understand and read correctly the "signs" of the times (4:6-11; 5:18-20; 6). Their lives reflected a total misunderstanding of what real religion required of the people of Israel (5:14-15, 21-24).

A second, and closely related, teaching centered in Amos's reinterpretation of the concept known as the "day of the LORD," which obviously was well known to the people of Israel. This idea probably derived from an older concept known as "holy war," when the god or gods assisted a people in battle. In a holy war all conquered people and property were to be killed or burned as sacrifice in honor of the god and in gratitude for the victory. (Examples of such instances may be found in various places in the Old Testament, especially Joshua 7 and 1 Samuel 15.) This older thinking had evolved into the idea that Yahweh was about to act in such a way as to destroy evil nations, which to the minds of the people of Israel naturally meant all nations *except* Israel. This coming time of judgment came to be known as the "day of Yahweh" or the "day of the LORD." Amos berated the people for looking forward to that day, however. Instead of judgment upon Israel's enemies, the primary judgment was to be directed against Israel herself. Since the people had become so unrighteous, God had no choice except to punish *his* people— those who ought to have known how to live and how to please God (5:18-20).

Another teaching of Amos which resounds throughout his oracles is that of responsibility, human responsibility to be and to live on the highest possible levels. The oracles against the foreign nations depicted judgment as coming upon those nations because they did not live up to their own principles and levels of acceptable behavior. Since Israel had enjoyed a special relationship with God and had been the recipient of God's special revelation, that nation would be judged even more harshly than others. The clear and simple teaching of Amos is that privilege begets responsibility.

> You only have I known
> of all the families of the earth;
> therefore I will punish you
> for all your iniquities.
> —3:2

The final and decisive teaching of Amos centered in the certain conviction that Israel was to be destroyed, never again to rise. There are those who attempt to detect in Amos's teaching some hope for the future, perhaps a remnant idea that a few would be spared from the invading army and from these few a new nation would evolve, but upon close examination of the text one finds no such hope. One recalls that the culture from which the Old Testament emerged basically viewed life in terms of corporate units or groups, *not* individual persons. Our own culture is so saturated with individualism that it is sometimes difficult for modern persons to understand that the group was the most important entity to ancient societies. The individual, while important to a degree, was important *only* as that person contributed to or detracted from the larger societal unit. Therefore, if a nation was basically evil, the nation would be destroyed, including individuals who were "good." To persons accustomed to thinking in terms of individual rights, this seems somewhat unfair. Unfair it may appear, but in the harsh reality of life things usually work in this manner. Innocent people quite frequently suffer because of the evils of others when judgment finally does fall on the offending group.

The Concept of the Remnant

There are several passages which have been cited in the attempt to find a remnant concept in Amos's teachings: 3:12; 5:3; and 9:8c-15, especially 9:9-10. Upon close examination, however, these passages do not support such an idea. The passage in 3:12 is found in the midst of a larger unit which is describing the fall of the nation, and it reflects a part of the culture of the time. When a shepherd who had been hired to tend the flocks reported to the owner of the flocks that a wild animal had killed one of the lambs, it was the accepted practice for the shepherd to bring the owner as much as could be rescued of the carcass. (Obviously this was the manner in which thievery was discouraged!) The animal was not saved, but the remnants were presented as evidence that the wild beast had killed it. So in 3:12 Amos used that particular figure to impress upon the people of Israel just how great the destruction of their land was going to be. "Two ankle bones and a piece of an ear" would not be much remaining from an entire lamb! The only evidence that Israel had ever existed would be "the corner of a couch and part of a bed." This certainly would not be a living remnant but only a grim reminder of how little would be left after God's judgment upon the proud nation had come.

The passage in 5:3 is likewise a graphic illustration of the future destruction and desolation of the people and land. Ninety percent would be destroyed. And the clear implication of Amos's teaching was that the remainder would be carried into exile. The totality of the destruction is evident throughout the entire collection of Amos' oracles (6:9; 7:8-9; 8:2; 9:1, 8ab).

The only real contradiction to the idea of total destruction is found in the conclusion to the book, 9:8c-15. These verses have been a battleground for scholars for many years, since they appear to contradict the clear message of Amos that God was going to destroy Israel "from the face of the earth." One of the first problems one finds in interpreting this passage concerns just how long the conclusion is: does it contain 9:8c-15 or 9:9-15 or 9:11-15? The most likely explanation is that 9:11-15 is a postexilic oracle placed here by the postexilic editors to show their hope and conviction that God would make of his people a nation again. It is clear, however, that the oracle in 9:11-15 is directed toward and reflects the nation of Judah. The reference to the "root of David" is definitely Judean, and the allusion to the increased fertility of the land is quite in keeping with postexilic thinking concerning the new age when the kingdom of David would be again restored. What this "happy" ending to Amos's teaching of doom reflects, then, is the attempt on the part of the postexilic editors to preserve the basic teachings of the prophet but also to use these teachings in such a way as to speak to the people who at that time needed to understand that there was hope after judgment.

Such editorial activity concerns some present-day interpreters of these materials. Their question revolves around which of the two teachings is historically accurate. That was not, however, a matter of great concern for the people of those times, for in reality both teachings were correct and true. Amos's proclamation of the complete destruction of Israel was absolutely correct—but the postexilic editors were also correct. God had restored his people in the land, and they looked forward to being a political entity once again. The nation of Israel *as such* would not be restored, however; but if one recalls the corporate thinking of the time, one can readily understand the idea that in the restoration of the people of God in the land a new Israel *had* emerged. The old message of Amos was then combined with a new message of hope both as a recollection of past events and also as a warning for the people of God in the future.

Some further discussion about Amos 9:8c-10 must take place to make the picture complete. After clearly stating that Israel was to be destroyed in 9:8ab, the reader is immediately struck with the comment in 9:8c, "except that I will not utterly destroy the house of Jacob." Because of the apparently abrupt change in teaching many scholars believe that 9:8c is the beginning of the "happy" ending appended in the postexilic period for reasons already given. The problem with this understanding, however, is that verses 9-10 appear to be an additional warning that the destruction will be complete. Why would the editors have made such an arrangement? One solution to the problem has been to interpret these verses as emphasizing that some will escape by taking the term "pebble" in 9:9 to refer to "good" people. But this solution is not very convincing since it seems clear that the entire section is referring to destruction rather than escape.

Another possible solution is to understand 9:8c as referring to the people of God and not to the nation of Israel. If one interprets the passage in this manner the meaning of 9:8-10 would be that Amos understood that God would totally destroy the nation of Israel but would not totally destroy his people. This in fact proved to be correct. Such an approach would make 9:11-15 the only postexilic portion to be added to Amos's teaching. No one solution to this passage, however, has won general acceptance among scholars.

Amos's Visions of Judgment

There is one other segment of the Book of Amos which must be considered. This involves the collection of visions which was used as the basis for chapters 7–9. The sequence begins with two visions which Amos saw and, after seeing them, interceded with God on behalf of the people. Two comments should be made here. First, far from receiving some type of psychological satisfaction from delivering oracles of doom against the people (as some have charged), the prophet identified himself with them and often pleaded their case before God. Secondly, here in the arrangement of the scenes is the same religious teaching already exhibited (4:6-12) which emphasized that God sent partial judgments in order that the people might recognize their sin and turn back to God. When it became evident that the nation was not going to repent and was far out of line with God's righteous requirements (7:7-9), Amos understood that the judgment was inevitable. This is clearly seen in the famous vision of the basket of summer fruit. As noted in the introduction, in Hebrew, a language written only with consonants (the vowels added by sound), the word "summer fruit" is spelled *qyts* (but pronounced *qayits*). When Amos saw the summer fruit, he also received a revelation or message from God. "The end has come upon my people Israel." The word "end" is also spelled in Hebrew *qyts* (but pronounced *qêts*). The last vision (9:1) is that of God standing beside the sacred altar proclaiming that the judgment must take place.

Amos was not a professional prophet. He had not been trained in the religious "schools" for this purpose. His understanding was that God had *called* him to do this duty, to perform this service. This is one of the chief characteristics of the great prophets. They did not believe that they spoke in their own names or with their own authority but in the name of Yahweh and with Yahweh's authority. The message was not the message *they* wanted to deliver but the one they were given by God.

Amos is the first of the prophets whose words are collected and preserved in a book. He is certainly not the last, however. How contemporary some of his sayings are! Are there instances today of religious hypocrisy in our society? How many people believe that prosperity *must* be the result of doing right in the religious sphere? Are there in our society examples of injustice in the courts (5:10-13), of extravagance in the face of hunger and want (3:15; 4:1; 6:4-6), of corrupt and deceitful business practices (2:6-7a; 8:4-6)? A society with such elements cannot long survive because it will crumble from the weight of its own oppressions and the decay of its moral foundation. Amos did not believe that changes should be made simply because society would be better because of them or because people owed such conduct to each other as people; this is a humanistic understanding. Rather, the changes which Amos proposed, even demanded, were changes which were rooted in his understanding of God. Any people who claimed to be the people of God were under obligation to act as God required, in accordance with God's nature and commandments. Probably the most famous and well-known of Amos's teachings reflects that basic idea:

I hate, I despise your feasts,
    and I take no delight in your solemn assemblies.
Even though you offer me your burnt offerings and cereal offerings,
    I will not accept them,
and the peace offerings of your fatted beasts,
    I will not look upon.
Take away from me the noise of your songs;
    to the melody of your harps I will not listen.
But let justice roll down like waters,
    and righteousness like an ever-flowing stream.

—5:20-24

HOSEA

Hosea was a prophet to Israel also but, unlike Amos, was a native of the Northern Kingdom. He appears to have exercised his prophetic ministry during the years 750–725 B.C.; this was for the most part a period of political instability in Israel. One recalls that Israel was defeated and overrun by the Assyrians in 732 B.C. and much of its territory was incorporated into the Assyrian Empire. When the Israelite king Hoshea rebelled in 727 B.C., the Assyrians came into the area, captured and destroyed Samaria, and carried most of the people into exile around 722 B.C. Clearly Hosea prophesied during a very trying historical moment.

There are several points which should be noted before turning to examine the text of Hosea *per se*. One of these concerns the marriage of this prophet. Scholars have argued for some time about the "woman problem" in Hosea. One learns from the text that Hosea married a woman who was a harlot. The question often argued is whether Gomer was a harlot before Hosea married her, or whether she became such a person after the marriage, or whether she may have been a woman who served her time in the practice of cultic prostitution. Some argue that every young woman had to serve as a cultic prostitute for a period of time as a religious duty. There is also disagreement on whether there is one woman depicted in chapters 1 and 3 or whether the text speaks of two different women. From a careful study of the text it seems unlikely that two different women are being described. It is clear that the stories were told to make the point that as Gomer was unfaithful to Hosea, so had Israel been unfaithful to Yahweh. The tragic elements in his life were understood by Hosea as "prophetic signs" (see p. 32).

A second consideration to be kept in mind in studying the Book of Hosea is that the original Hebrew text is in terrible condition. This is not to say that the overall message of the book cannot be understood, but it is necessary to point out that the text of Hosea is one of the least well preserved of all the Old Testament documents. At points the text is almost impossible to translate and/or to make sense of, making precise interpretation very difficult.

Finally the basic teaching of Hosea lies in his contention that the problem with the people of Israel was that they did not "know" Yahweh, in other words, they were not in the proper relationship with God. (The word "know" in the Old Testament usually signifies not intellectual knowledge but rather personal relationship, and frequently relationships of a most intimate type.) Hosea understood that this sorry condition resulted from the fact that Israel had broken the covenant made between God and the people. In Hebrew the word for "loyalty to the covenant" is ḥesed, quite frequently translated as love, mercy, or steadfast love. (The letter "h" with a dot under it stands for one of the two "h" sounds in the Hebrew alphabet. This one may be pronounced simply as an "h," but it is more precise to pronounce this "h" with a panting sound.) The idea contained within the word, however, connotes loyalty and obligation rather than emotional feeling. Many interpreters have taken the translation of ḥesed as "love" and attempted to make of Hosea the great prophet of love. While there is in Hosea's teaching an element of compassion and deep feeling, it would be misleading to understand his teaching as simply that of love in the sentimental and emotional sense. Whatever else Hosea taught, he proclaimed very pointedly that the people of Israel had violated their covenant obligation with God and would be destroyed because of the violation. There are some hope passages in the book; however, how much hope is Hosea's and how much belongs to the final postexilic editors must be determined by an examination of each passage.

Study Outline for the Book of Hosea

I. (Auto) Biographical Material: 1–3
II. Oracles About Israel: 4–14

(Auto) Biographical Material

The Book of Hosea begins with a collection of materials which tell the reader something about the prophet's life and how that life enabled Hosea to understand more fully Israel's relationship with God. His children were given symbolic names which should be understood as prophetic signs: *Jezreel*, a place of war and destruction; *Lo-ruhamah* (not-pitied) because of the constant and continuous sin of the nation; and *Lo-ammi* (not my people) to demonstrate that judgment does come and the covenant can be annulled. It is interesting to note that chapter 1 is a prose narrative in the third person and chapter 3 a prose narrative in the first person. Chapter 2 is a poetic composition depicting the relationship between God and Israel similar to that of a faithful husband and a wandering wife.

One of the more interesting problems of this section concerns the passages which seem to reflect the possibility of restoration. In 2:14-15 and 3:1-5, specifically, there are elements of hope, but whether this hope came from the postexilic editors or from Hosea cannot be determined with certainty. Further discussion of the hope teachings will be continued later.

Oracles

The remainder of the book consists of oracles directed against

Israel; there are no oracles against foreign nations in this collection. As one reads these sayings, one is struck with the sophistication and wit of the prophet, so much so that some interpreters believe Hosea to have been a part of the wisdom movement. He used many short pithy sayings, figures of speech in making comparisons, and wordplay; his sense of humor and irony is fascinating. For example, at one point he ironically depicts Israel as dying with the vulture already circling overhead (8:1).

Hosea understood, as did Amos, the fundamental problem of the nation as a religious one. Israel had broken the covenant relationship with God, and this rupture affected not only the people's relationship with God but the people's relationship with one another. Human relationships were a reflection of what had gone wrong between the people and God; there was a broken relationship attributable to the careless attitude the people demonstrated toward *hesed*, covenant loyalty:

> There is no faithfulness or kindness,
>   and no knowledge of God in the land;
> there is swearing, lying, killing,
>   stealing and committing adultery;
> they break all bounds and murder
>   follows murder.
>
> —4:1c-2

The reason for this "lack of knowledge" lay largely, according to Hosea, in the failure of the religious leaders to display proper religious teaching and moral conduct in their own lives. Religious ritual with no corresponding moral content cannot be a substitute for *hesed* and knowledge of God. The proper motions will not insure proper relationship with the deity. Perhaps the most well-known saying of Hosea, and the one which most pointedly demonstrates his basic teaching, is found in 6:6:

> For I desire *hesed* [covenant loyalty] and not sacrifice,
>   the knowledge of God, rather than burnt offerings.

Hosea believed that Assyria would be the instrument of God's judgment on the nation Israel; Amos had not known exactly whom God would use, but he knew that it would be either Assyria or Egypt (Amos 3:9). By the time of Hosea, the executioner had become rather plain.

Hope Passages

The most intriguing and controversial of all the problems connected with Hosea's teaching revolves around the hope passages found in the book. Some older scholars assigned any hope passages to postexilic editors; others attempted to make of Hosea a slushy sentimentalist. Perhaps the truth lies, as usual, somewhere in between. Upon a close reading of the text one senses as deep and caring a concern on the part of Hosea for the people as he had felt for his wayward wife. But the basic thrust of his teaching remained that God was going to destroy Israel. What kind of hope can one find in the agonies of this sensitive man? A study of two passages may be helpful.

The first passage is chapter 3. One of the issues debated (as noted before) is whether the woman in chapter 3 is the same as the woman in chapter 1. If the intent was to portray the same woman, there may here be a teaching that after the judgment would come a restoration of the relationship between God and Israel. If, however, the woman in chapter 3 refers to someone other than Gomer, the teaching would seem to indicate that the restoration would have to occur with some other nation. Since David is plainly mentioned in chapter 3, some argue that the editors were using this second story to speak to the postexilic community which had been restored in Judah. It is quite possible that this assessment is correct, but certainty cannot be assured in the interpretation of this passage.

The second section of interest is found in chapter 11 where Hosea movingly depicts God and Israel in a parent-child relationship. God reflected on his nurture of Israel (comparing it to teaching a child to walk) and its subsequent deliberate and systematic breaking of the covenant relationship. Despite God's attempts to restore that relationship, Israel rejected him. Because of this sin, judgment had to come. The crucial verse is 11:9:

> I will not execute my fierce anger,
>   I will not again destroy Ephraim;
> for I am God and not man,
>   the Holy One in your midst,
>   and I will not come to destroy.

The interpretation of this passage is difficult indeed, partly because of the state of the text of Hosea. Some argue that the reference to "again destroying Ephraim" is clear support for the idea that the passage is postexilic, that it presupposes the first destruction of Israel. This is a quite legitimate understanding of the text. It is also possible to interpret the text somewhat differently, however. Close examination of the passage reveals that the restoration of the *nation* is not what is basically at issue, but rather the restoration of the *covenant*. This covenant was understood to have originated in the wilderness wanderings. It is interesting to note that the last line of the passage reads literally in the Hebrew, "I will not come into the city." This translation, together with the emphasis upon the covenant and wilderness, could mean that, even though the nation would not be restored, God could enter into another relationship with the people wherever they were. Such would occur, however, apart from the nation as a political entity (symbolized by the "city"). Yahweh could still be their God during their wanderings from the land just as in the days when the Hebrew people were nomads without settled roots. This idea may also be reflected in 12:9:

> I am the LORD your God
>   from the land of Egypt;
> I will again make you dwell in tents,
>   as in the days of the appointed feast.

These passages of hope, while probably altered somewhat in the transmission of the material, are most likely derived originally from Hosea's teachings. The last of the hope passages (14:4-8), however, is almost universally accepted to be a postexilic oracle placed here by the postexilic editors to speak to the restored community. One notes with interest that the hope is nevertheless followed by a stern warning that any return to idolatry would carry serious consequences.

Hosea learned from the tragedies of his own life something about the pain God experiences when human beings break his covenant and turn their backs upon him. How many persons today can learn from similar experiences involving the breaking of covenants—in marriage as well as in other areas? One of the fundamental problems of modern society lies in the cavalier attitude people have toward keeping their covenant word. The teaching of Hosea can also serve to demonstrate that no matter how much compassion and care may be lavished upon a person or group or nation, there may be no hope for a change in that one's mode of behavior and action. In short, all the love in the world may not be able to redeem someone or some group. That is a shocking and frightening thought, but according to the teaching of Hosea, it is true. If so, how does that concept affect some of our modern thinking about certain relationships in our society (marriage and divorce, law and justice, etc.)?

ISAIAH 1–39

The Book of Isaiah stands first in the Hebrew collection of prophetic scrolls. An examination of the book reveals that it is not simply a collection of the oracles of the prophet Isaiah who lived in the eighth century B.C. It is, rather, a book comprised of several units of tradition, each of which had its own specific historical context. The Book of Isaiah, then, illustrates how the prophetic tradition was remembered, passed along, and reinterpreted to fit new historical settings. In the process new sayings were fashioned by those who revered and preserved the tradition. Some scholars like to call such a group a "school." This may not be the most appropriate term to use to designate this phenomenon, but it makes one aware that the teachings of a particular prophet were passed along by those who honored his words. And it further illustrates that such groups not only passed along the "old words" but also attempted to make those words relevant to each specific period of history. The preservers of the tradition sought to understand the spirit of the prophet in such a way as to feel confident that new teachings which one or more of the group espoused would be in keeping with the mind of the great teacher of the past.

It has often been understood by interpreters of the prophetic materials in particular that, if the teachings of a prophet presuppose a specific historical setting, one assumes that the prophet spoke at that time. This understanding is very important in dealing with the material in the Book of Isaiah. Most of the material found in Isaiah 1–39 presupposes the historical period of the eighth century with kings Uzziah, Ahaz, and Hezekiah as the rulers of Judah, and the Assyrian Empire as the most powerful nation of the time. It is only logical to assume that Isaiah spoke during that time.

But the remaining material in chapters 40–66 does not presuppose that period of history. Chapters 40–55, for example, reflect a time when the people of Judah were in exile in Babylon shortly before the Persian king, Cyrus, conquered Babylonia. It seems reasonable to assume that the prophet who spoke those words was among the captives in Babylon around 550–540 B.C. And, finally, chapters 56–66 presuppose an historical setting in the postexilic community in Judah during the trying times when the new temple had been rebuilt. It again seems logical to understand that the prophet(s) who delivered the oracles of 56–66 was a member of that postexilic community in approximately 520–450 B.C.

One may indeed be puzzled as to why those who edited the Book of Isaiah would collect all of these sayings from different persons and different historical settings into one book under the same name. This phenomenon, however, did not seem at all unusual to the Hebrew mindset. Quite frequently the founder of (or even the most famous person of) a "movement" would be understood as the embodiment of the entire movement. Often all aspects of that movement were attributed to the founder even if many of the ideas developed later. For example, Moses was the first great lawgiver of Israel; therefore, all laws go back to Moses, even those which developed later. David was the first to popularize and emphasize the writing of psalms; therefore, all psalms are in some way connected with David. Solomon was the first to legitimate wisdom in Israel's history; therefore, it was understood that all wisdom in some way went back to Solomon. This same phenomenon occurred in the compilation of the Book of Isaiah. The prophet of the eighth century was so influential that his teachings were especially revered and preserved; those who preserved them continued to speak to the people in times of crisis as if it were Isaiah who was speaking. This type of understanding may be strange to us, but it was indeed commonplace to the people of that time.

At this point, therefore, the discussion will be limited to an investigation of chapters 1–39 of the Book of Isaiah, because these chapters incorporate, for the most part, the teachings of the Isaiah who lived in the eighth century B.C. This quite influential man appears to have been a native of Jerusalem, a highly educated person who served as a court counselor to kings. There is also some evidence that he may have been a member of the priesthood. His prophetic ministry covered a long period of time beginning in the days of King Uzziah (ca. 742 B.C.) and continuing until the reign of Hezekiah was over (ca. 687–686 B.C.). The tradition (from a much later time and not authenticated, however) about his death was that he was sawn in two during the reign of Manasseh.

Like Amos and Hosea, the prophet Isaiah's teachings were characterized by one major theme around which other sub-themes revolved. Isaiah's teaching focused on the concept of faith, perhaps better understood as faithfulness or trust in God. The basic idea in this teaching was that the people were to trust Yahweh. Part of that process involved the entrusting or commitment of their lives to God. Such a commitment insured that whenever this happened there would be genuine religion, a right relationship with God. One notes immediately that, even though Amos, Hosea, and Isaiah had different thrusts to their teachings, the end result they had in mind was exactly the same—that the people be in the proper relationship with God, which would make their lives different from ordinary human existence.

Isaiah's emphasis on faith in God was grounded in his understanding of Yahweh as a great and majestic being who was "holy." His favorite expression to designate God was "The Holy One of Israel." The term "holy" in the Hebrew language did not originally connote ethical morality, but it implied something as being "other than." God was holy because God was "other than" or "separate from" the created order and the human race. Isaiah understood God as holy because He was exalted, magnificent, and apart from human existence and understanding.

There is one additional motif found in Isaiah's teachings, the one for which the prophet is perhaps most well-known. This teaching has to do with a messiah. Unfortunately, most persons do not really understand the concept of messiah as it emerged in the prophetic teachings, especially in the Book of Isaiah. The word "messiah" in Hebrew means literally "anointed one." Thus anyone who was anointed to perform a particular function could be understood as a "messiah." In those days there were three groups of persons whose numbers could be anointed (set apart for a special function): prophets, priests, and kings. At the time of the great prophets the most usual ceremony involving anointing was the anointing of the king. During the period of the monarchy, therefore, there came to be a major emphasis on the king as Yahweh's anointed. This was especially true during periods when there was a bad king. In such times the prophets began to look forward to a new and better period brought about by a new and better ruler. The idea seems to have originated in Judah, where the emphasis would understandably have been on a king from the lineage of David. Messianism began, therefore, as a religio-political idea.

Study Outline for the Book of Isaiah 1–39

  I. Collection of Material, Oracles and Narrative: 1–12
      A. Introduction to the entire collection: 1
      B. Oracles from Isaiah's earlier ministry: 2–4
      C. God and people: 5–11
         Call of Isaiah: 6
      D. Concluding oracles: 12
  II. Oracles Against Foreign Nations: 13–23
 III. Doom and Hope Oracles: 24–35
      A. Postexilic collection: 24–27
      B. Sayings of Isaiah: 28–33
      C. Doom on Edom, hope for Zion: 34–35
 IV. Historical Narratives: 36–39

The collection in Isaiah 1–39 follows a pattern which seems to have been set for each of the longer prophetic books: oracles against the nation; oracles against foreign nations; hope passages (sometimes blended with narratives about the prophet); and a historical conclusion. The material contained in these chapters is basically related to the career of Isaiah of the eighth century. There are a few exceptions, however, two of which will be mentioned more explicitly later.

Basic Teaching

Most of the teaching of Isaiah is contained in chapters 1–12. One can learn much about the way in which the prophetic editors worked by examining these chapters. For example, the heart of the section, perhaps even of the entire collection 1–39, appears to be located in 6:1–9:7. This segment begins with the call of Isaiah and contains several episodes from his life, providing a clear historical setting for the prophet and his work. It also forms the focus for the oracles of Isaiah which are preserved both before and after this section. It is interesting to note that this section interrupts the flow of another collection, beginning with 5:1-30 and continuing in 9:8-21. There are other groups of sayings which appear to be collections of oracles designed either by theme (i.e., hope, sin, judgment, etc.) or by "catchwords" (key words in oracles which are the same even though the overall message of the different oracles may be different; this was a quite common way of arranging material in those days). Sometimes the two elements are combined.

The first chapter of Isaiah is arranged around a common theme, the sin of the people and God's judgment upon them unless they repent. One of the more familiar passages from the Book of Isaiah is found in this chapter:

> Come now, let us reason together,
>   says the LORD:
> though your sins are like scarlet,
>   shall they become as white as snow?
> though they are red like crimson,
>   shall they become like wool?
> If you are willing and obedient,
>   you shall eat the good of the land;
> But if you refuse and rebel,
>   you shall be devoured by the sword;
>   for the mouth of the LORD has spoken.
>   —1:18-20 (paraphrased)

These verses reflect Isaiah's basic teachings to the people. The people of Judah were not as deeply enmeshed in sin as the Northern Kingdom had been. There was some hope for Judah to escape destruction if the people would be obedient to Yahweh and would remain faithful. If they did not, the judgment would indeed come. Isaiah did predict, however, that the anger of Yahweh would bring some, but not total, destruction to the land. This occurred when the Assyrians overran the countryside around 701 B.C. capturing forty-six walled cities, and surrounding Jerusalem. Parts of chapters 2–4, plus 5:24-30 and 9:8–10:11, seem to describe some of those events.

Isaiah's Prophetic Activity

As already indicated, the most important segment of Isaiah

1–39 is the material collected together in 6:1–9:7. Here are some of the most important episodes in Isaiah's ministry. First, there is the call experience (chapter 6). This type of experience was an important element in the careers of most of the prophets, for each of them felt a definite summons by God to serve as his messenger. A call account for every prophet has not survived, however. Isaiah's call came during a ceremony in the temple in Jerusalem. The account is related in another example of "theophany" (see pp. 34-35). The fact that this occurred in the temple has led some scholars to think that Isaiah may have been a priest, although any profession other than prophet cannot be demonstrated unequivocally.

The primary question relating to this episode revolves around the purpose of the call. If one simply took at face value the reason given for the call, one would be left in great bewilderment. The clear teaching is that Isaiah was called to speak to the people for the purpose of establishing them (or making them firm) in their sin so that their judgment would be assured. This seems rather unusual to contemporary persons who usually interpret the message of God to be a call to repentance so that judgment may be *escaped*. In Old Testament thought patterns, however, there was not the same kind of clear line drawn between purpose and result. Their reasoning went something like this: if an event occurred, then it must have had a purpose; whatever result came to pass must then have been intended; since Judah was warned and did not ultimately repent and thus was destroyed, the prophetic preaching must have been intended to bring about that result—i.e., destruction. What Isaiah was called to do was to preach to the nation concerning its sin, to urge repentance, and to warn that judgment would surely come unless changes were made. When the people did not ultimately repent, the judgment came—a validation to the thinking of that era that Isaiah had spoken the true word of God.

A second major segment of this portion of Isaiah (beginning in chapter 7) contains a series of stories concerning Isaiah and his relationship with King Ahaz when the king was considering appealing to Assyria for assistance at the time of the Syro-Ephraimitic alliance. One recalls that the prophets discouraged political alliances because the inferior state had to promise not only a substantial tribute to the superior but had to erect places of worship for the gods of that nation. To the religious purist in Judah this was idolatry. Isaiah counseled Ahaz not to appeal to Assyria because the prophet believed that Yahweh would use Assyria to destroy both Syria and Israel. Judah would then escape without any commitments, either financial or religious.

The most famous and highly controversial passage in the Book of Isaiah is found in this section, 7:10-17. Here Isaiah told Ahaz that Yahweh would deliver the land of Judah, and as a guarantee told Ahaz to ask for a sign. Ahaz, his mind already made up, refused to do this, whereupon Isaiah gave him a sign anyway, found in 7:14. The literal translation of this Hebrew text is as follows:

> Behold, the young woman is pregnant
> and is about to bear a son
> and you shall call his name Immanuel.
> —7:14 (author's translation)

One notes that this is not a prediction of someone to come in the distant future but a specific concrete event to take place within a few months. Isaiah went on to say that before the child would know how to "refuse the evil and choose the good, the land before whose two kings you are in dread will be deserted" (7:16). The meaning of the text is very clear. There is a woman standing near Isaiah and Ahaz (Isaiah's wife? perhaps Ahaz's wife?) who was already far along in her pregnancy. Isaiah told Ahaz that before the child was old enough to know the difference between right and wrong (in those days somewhere between two and twelve years old) Israel and Syria would be destroyed. This encounter between Isaiah and Ahaz occurred ca. 734 B.C. In 732 B.C. Syria was destroyed and Israel weakened, and in 722–721 B.C. Israel was completely defeated. Isaiah's prediction was absolutely correct! The name given to the child was intended as one of those prophetic signs, Immanuel, meaning "God is with us." The emphasis in this passage (and in a companion passage, 8:1-5) is upon God's action to deliver his people from danger. And that deliverance came to pass.

The Messianic Hope

When there was a bad king, as in this period, there obviously arose the longing on the part of some of the religious leaders

and perhaps even the people for a new king who would lead
the people in the proper paths and be faithful to God. Naturally
this idealized king came to be understood as a new David, partly
because the king would come from the Davidic line and partly
because David had been idealized by this time. He was perceived
as a man of God who governed the people like a shepherd,
made just decisions, and strengthened the country. One cannot
help but recall just how many "warts" David really had (2
Samuel 9–20); but so did Washington, Jefferson, Lincoln, and
many of our American national heroes! Yet our history books
tend to idealize them. Isaiah looked forward to a new and better
king, an anointed one, who would lead the people as God
wanted—not as Ahaz had done. There are two passages which
reflect this hope, one in 9:2-7 and the other in chapter 11.

Scholars argue about when the idea of a messiah originated
in Israelite religious thought. Some argue that the idea was a
postexilic development exclusively; others believe that the historical situation in preexilic times was more appropriate for the
origin of such an idea. The latter position is the one advocated
here because the messianic idea fits most appropriately into the
preexilic historical setting. This does not mean, however, that
the postexilic editors may not have embellished the traditions
at certain points.

The passage in 9:2-7 is quite probably Isaiah's teaching re-
flecting his hope that there actually would be a new king in
Judah loyal to Yahweh. Some scholars have argued that this
oracle may have been delivered by Isaiah on the occasion of the
birth of Hezekiah as a prophetic sign to insure that he would
be a good king. Others argue, perhaps more correctly, that the
oracle may have been delivered on the occasion of Hezekiah's
ascent to the throne, for the names in 9:6 and the description
of his reign given in 9:7 are typical designations for a king of
that time. Hezekiah did prove to be a good king, religiously
speaking.

The description given in chapter 11, however, is much more
debated by scholars. Many interpreters believe that this oracle
was a product of the postexilic period, basing much of their
argument on the reference in 11:1 to the "stump of Jesse." This
could be interpreted as a reference to the fact that there was no
Davidic king at that moment and would certainly reflect the

historical period of the exilic and postexilic periods. The word "stump," in Hebrew, however, may be also translated as "stalk" or "stem," which would not necessarily imply that the Davidic kingship was nonexistent at the time. If this latter interpretation is accepted, the time in all probability would be preexilic. The passage itself is so very much Isaianic in its content that it is difficult to deny categorically that the teaching originated with Isaiah. It may have been edited slightly from the postexilic perspective, however.

One of the more famous biblical quotations is found within this passage:

> The wolf shall dwell with the lamb,
>   and the leopard shall lie down with the kid,
> and the calf and the lion and the fatling together,
>   and a little child shall lead them.
> The cow and the bear shall feed;
>   their young shall lie down together;
>   and the lion shall eat straw like the ox.
> The sucking child shall play over the hole of the asp,
>   and the weaned child shall put his hand on the adder's den.
> They shall not hurt or destroy in all my holy mountain;
> for the earth shall be full of the knowledge of the LORD
>   as the waters cover the sea.
>
> —11:6-9

These verses have usually been understood to refer to a future utopian paradise. That is a possible interpretation, but more in keeping with the time of Isaiah would be to understand the wild animals as symbols for nations (as we frequently do today) and to interpret the passage as Isaiah's hope for a period of real peace in his time. In all interpretations one must remember that the prophets are poets, and poetry must not be made into narrative history.

Of all the historical incidents which occurred during Isaiah's ministry, the dramatic withdrawal of Sennacherib's army from around Jerusalem was the best remembered. Isaiah had told Hezekiah that Yahweh would not allow the Assyrians to capture the city—and they did not. This marvelous deliverance gradually came to be understood by the people as God's assurance that Jerusalem was his city and that he would not ever allow it to be destroyed, a hope that was to be rudely shattered later on. The editors of this portion of Isaiah structured the material to point toward such a destruction, however, for the final chapter of this portion of Isaiah (39) looks forward to the coming exile at the hands of the Babylonians.

Postexilic Materials

There are two other portions of chapters 1–39 which deserve some special comment. These sections are 24–27 and 34–35. It is almost universally accepted among Old Testament scholars that chapters 24–27 are a separate entity and that these chapters are from the postexilic period. The content of the material reflects the time of the restored community in Judah, but an exact date for these passages cannot be agreed upon. Dates range all the way from 520 B.C. to 200 B.C., and almost every era within that time span has some advocates. The truth is that a certain answer cannot be obtained for this puzzle. It appears that the materials are diverse, probably originating at different times and in differing historical situations.

Several points should be emphasized. The first is that the tone of the entire section is set by the threat of God's judgment on a large portion of the world. This activity by God would assist the postexilic community in Judah to become a major power and force in the world community. Further, there is a major emphasis on the destruction of a city (25:1-2), but the identity of the city is not made known to the reader. It obviously refers to a city which had been the focal point for some type of oppression of the people in the restored community.

The third element in these chapters worthy of attention focuses on certain ideas and vocabulary which were associated with the later apocalyptic movement (see p. 96). Most of this material is found in chapters 26–27, and there is in 26:19 a reference to resurrection, an idea which developed late in the history of Hebrew religious thought. Scholars, however, are not really certain how the passage should be understood. Is it simply a figurative poetic comment used to illustrate a point? Or is it specifically a doctrine of resurrection? And if so, does it refer to the resurrection of individuals or of the corporate nation?

If this passage does refer to the resurrection of individuals, it seems strange that no further comment is made about this idea. More than likely the reference is to be understood as a poetic description of the restored community, similar to the idea in Ezekiel's valley of dry bones (Ezekiel 37). There are several references in these chapters to the exiles in Babylon returning to Judah. These chapters would be best studied along with the material found in the postexilic prophetic books, especially Isaiah 40–55, 56–66, Zechariah 9–14, and perhaps Joel.

Chapters 34 and 35 comprise another segment of Isaiah 1–39 which need some further explication. Most scholars are agreed that these chapters should be dated later than the eighth-century Isaiah. Many believe that both chapters should be assigned to the great prophet of the Exile whose teachings are collected together in Isaiah 40–55 (see pp. 86-94). Upon close examination, however, it appears that chapter 34 deals with the destruction of some of the enemies of God's people, especially Edom, which would insure the continuation of God's people in the land. Such an oracle appears to be more appropriately placed in the post-exilic period when the restored community was experiencing difficulties with surrounding peoples who were threatening their very existence. Perhaps Isaiah 34 would be more appropriately studied with the prophetic book of Obadiah (see pp. 107, 108).

Chapter 35 appears to belong to the teachings of the great prophet during the Exile in Babylon who proclaimed to the people that they would soon be released and be allowed to return to Judah. That time was viewed as a new Exodus wherein the desert would blossom and God would lead the people home on a specially prepared pathway. This is clearly the teaching of this chapter, and it would be best to study it along with Isaiah 40 (see pp. 86-94).

The Continuing Message of Isaiah

It is easy to understand why the teaching of the eighth-century Isaiah was so revered by the religious community of Jerusalem. Isaiah's emphasis upon the majesty and power of God and God's relationship with his people had a twofold implication: God would judge any evil nation, including Judah, and would deliver his own people when that was appropriate. The means of deliverance could come in various forms—new and committed rulers, the destruction of enemy forces, even the lengthening of the life of a good leader. Isaiah's emphasis upon repentance before a situation had progressed too far was quite appropriate for that period of history. Judah had not yet gone beyond the point of no return in her evil ways as Israel had; therefore, if Judah wanted to be delivered, there was still time to repent.

Isaiah's challenge to the people of any age remains essentially the same as that which he delivered to his own people centuries ago. His call to trust God and entrust one's life to God is always valid. In fact, there can really be no religious experience apart from such a commitment. His understanding of the majesty and greatness of God is inspiring even today.

Two of Isaiah's teachings are perhaps most applicable for present times. The first centers in the idea that for a nation to be great, it must have great political leaders, persons of wisdom, integrity, morality, and principle. Quite frequently people in our society complain about "the government" as if it were only an impersonal system. A system it certainly is, but that system is managed by people (elected representatives in our society) whose principles and integrity guide their oversight and application of the system. There are certain systems which may be better than other systems, but none of them will function properly and fairly if the wrong persons are in control. Isaiah hoped for a better king. Doesn't our society have an advantage here in that we can elect our leaders? Instead of simply voting for persons who happen to want to run, could a system be developed whereby the best people are sought out and encouraged to aspire to public office? Since none will be perfect, however, the realization that mistakes will be made must be an accepted part of the package. Even the good king Hezekiah made some serious blunders.

Perhaps the second most contemporary application of Isaiah's teaching is the challenge to a nation (and individuals as well) to be aware constantly that unseemly modes of behavior may escape punishment for a time but will ultimately fall under judgment. Repentance is God's gift to people and society so that mistakes can be corrected. If warnings are ignored, however, there will come a time when the judgment will be most severe. There is a point of no return in human actions and activities both for groups and individuals.

MICAH

The prophet Micah was a Judean who lived in the countryside southwest of Jerusalem. He appears to have been a contemporary both of Hosea (for a short period) and of Isaiah for a longer time. It is probable that his ministry was influenced most significantly by the historical events of the reigns of Ahaz and Hezekiah.

Micah was primarily interested in speaking to the nations of Israel and Judah. He deeply believed that both would be punished for their transgressions, and both actually suffered judgment during his lifetime. Israel, in fact, ceased to exist as a nation at this time, and the people never returned. To this prophet the basic sin of the nations lay in the two capital cities, Samaria and Jerusalem. Some interpreters argue that this type of thinking was a result of the fact that Micah was from the rural area, making the cities a natural target for his preaching. That interpretation may be a bit too simple, however, since Micah's finger pointed the blame for the nations' sins primarily at the leaders—political, social, and religious. Since the leaders naturally made their headquarters in the capital cities, it may be, therefore, that Micah's enmity toward the cities came as a result of the fact that corrupt leadership was centered there rather than because of his rural background.

As for the arrangement of the book, there seem to be four basic sections alternating between denunciation and hope. Perhaps the contents of no other prophetic book have been as highly debated as these, for many scholars argue that the only authentic oracles from the man Micah are to be found in chapters 1–3. The remainder, they believe, came from other voices in other times. More will be said about this matter in the discussion of the material.

Study Outline for the Book of Micah

   I. Oracles of Doom: 1–3
   II. Modified Hope for the Future: 4–5
   III. Why the Nation Deserves Judgment: 6:1–7:6
   IV. Hope for a Future Restoration: 7:7-20

A large part of the first three chapters consists of oracles of doom against both Israel and Judah, primarily Judah. Specific passages are directed toward the leaders who were responsible

for exploiting the people of the land and for leading them astray.
A most dramatic oracle is found in 3:1-3:

> Hear, you heads of Jacob,
>   and rulers of the house of Israel!
> Is it not for you to know justice?—
>   You who hate the good and love the evil,
> who tear the skin from off my people,
>   and their flesh from off their bones;
> Who eat the flesh of my people,
>   and flay their skin from off them,
> And break their bones in pieces,
>   and chop them up like meat in a kettle,
>   like flesh in a caldron.

Micah predicted that Jerusalem would be destroyed (3:12).
While this event did not happen during Micah's lifetime, it did
occur later. Interestingly enough, this prediction about Jerusalem saved the life of Jeremiah during that prophet's ministry
(Jeremiah 26:16-19).

The second major section of the Book of Micah (4–5) contains
basically hope passages, material which has been assigned by
many interpreters to the postexilic period. There is evidence
which suggests that these teachings have been edited with a
postexilic perspective, but there are also some strong arguments
to support the idea that Micah was responsible for most of these
sayings. Since Micah's ministry lasted into the reign of Hezekiah,
it is quite possible that he initially held out great hope for Hezekiah's reform movement. A point in favor of this argument is
the fact that there are two similar oracles found in Isaiah and
Micah which could very easily be fitted into the historical setting
of their times, perhaps after the departure of the Assyrians from
the land in 701 B.C.

> For out of Zion shall go forth the law,
>   and the word of the LORD from Jerusalem.
> He shall judge between many peoples,
>   and shall decide for strong nations afar off;
> And they shall beat their swords into plowshares,
>   and their spears into pruning hooks;
> Nation shall not lift up sword against nation,
>   neither shall they learn war any more.
>   —4:2b-3 and Isaiah 2:3c-4

A second similarity between Isaiah and Micah is that both

looked forward to a better king from the lineage of David. This motif has already been examined in the teaching of Isaiah, and a similar idea is contained in Micah 5:2-4, another of those passages thought to be "messianic." The reference to the origin of the person in Bethlehem, however, is simply a reflection of the fact that this was traditionally understood to be David's home.

The third section of the book is 6:1–7:7, which deals with the sins of the people. It is in this section that one of the most famous of all the prophetic passages is located. There is in 6:1-8 a special literary type called the *Rîb*. This type is legal in nature and usually depicts someone bringing a charge against someone else in the setting of a court. In this passage the setting has Yahweh bringing his complaint against the people of Judah. The created order is called upon to act as a jury and to render a fair appraisal of the evidence. As usual in such instances there is a brief recital of what God had done for the people throughout their history and an implied challenge to respond aright to such graciousness. In 6:6-8 the prophet, speaking for the people and to the people, enumerates what had been substituted for genuine religious practice. At that point the prophet makes explicit what God requires of truly religious people.

> He has showed you, O man, what is good;
>   and what does the LORD require of you
>   but to do justice, and to love kindness, [*ḥesed*, covenant loyalty]
>   and to walk humbly with your God?

The last segment of the book, 7:8-20, definitely reflects the time of the Exile and after. The nation had been destroyed, but there was hope that the people would be restored in their land. Yahweh would forgive the people; this the postexilic community needed desperately to hear.

The message of the Book of Micah is quite similar to that of Isaiah 1–39. Sinfulness on the part of the leadership in all areas of life, political and religious, leads to a society that is unjust at best and may even approach repression and atrocity. Such a structure does not deserve to exist, and such leaders are simply despicable and insufferable.

Micah's warnings that these evils stand under God's justice should cause great searchings of heart among contemporary leadership, both political and ecclesiastical. His teachings, as

Isaiah's, should encourage people to seek out good leaders of high moral character and support them as they attempt to perform difficult tasks and make fair and just decisions. The hope of Micah that the nations should not learn war any more is a hope even today. If his description of what Yahweh requires of human beings were heeded and followed, the world might come closer to achieving that hope.

ZEPHANIAH

During the reign of Manasseh (beginning 687/6 B.C.), which lasted for about forty-five years, one hears no prophetic voice. Many scholars believe that there must have been a systematic persecution of the prophets of Yahweh during that period because Manasseh's reign was considered by the religious historians of Judah to have been the worst in the history of that nation. Whatever the cause, there is no known prophetic voice which can be traced to that period of Judah's history.

With the religious reform movement of Josiah, however, the climate became much more conducive to the development of the prophetic message. Out of this time came the voices of several prophets, the first of which is usually thought to have been that of Zephaniah. Most scholars date this prophet in the earlier years of Josiah's reign, around 630 B.C., just before the reform movement began. Some have conjectured that Zephaniah may even have been at least partially responsible for the initiation of the reform. There are a few scholars, however, who believe that Zephaniah's ministry would be more appropriately placed after the death of Josiah in the early years of Jehoiakim's reign (ca. 609 B.C.) when it had become apparent to everyone of religious sensitivity that the reform movement was dead. Zephaniah may then have been a contemporary of Jeremiah. Either the earlier or the later date would be acceptable for Zephaniah's ministry.

Study Outline for the Book of Zephaniah

I. Oracles Against Judah: 1:1–2:3
II. Oracles Against Foreign Nations: 2:4–3:8
III. Oracles of Hope and Restoration: 3:9-20

By now the student of the prophetic literature can immediately recognize the arrangement typical of the prophetic books even in this short collection of oracles. There are the oracles against the nation, against foreign nations, and those of hope and restoration. Several motifs characterize the teaching of this prophet. The reader is struck with the fact that the old concept of the "day of Yahweh" has been revived, and the meaning is essentially the same as Amos had given it. God's judgment was to come upon the people of God—and soon (1:14).

The prophet Zephaniah encountered a people who obviously had become rather indifferent to religious matters. They "do not seek the LORD or inquire of him" (1:6b); they had reached a point where they had no real conception of the power of God in life, "The LORD will not do good, nor will he do ill" (1:12c). They had become rather "secularized" for that time. The prophet was direct in his proclamation that the day of the LORD was about to befall them, and his description of the judgment is quite graphic (1:14-18).

Zephaniah, despite all his proclamations of doom, does seem to have held out some faint hope for the nation. He obviously believed that after the judgment a remnant of people would be left in the land. From this group, presumed by Zephaniah to be those who were meek and humble, would come the nucleus for a new community of God's people. The concluding portion of the book shows again the definite postexilic flavor of restoration after judgment.

While the Book of Zephaniah is short, it nevertheless exhibits both the typical preexilic elements of judgment on the people, with an appropriate recitation of their sins, and the particular emphases of the prophet. Two may be highlighted for special consideration for our times. There is, first of all, the charge against the people of Judah that they had become quite secularized. No one believed that God had any real interest in the affairs of the nations of the world or that, even if he did, there was any possibility that God would intervene in the ongoing affairs of human history. Decisions were made and lives were lived as if God did not exist. To a certain degree this is a reflection of our own time.

The second especially appropriate emphasis is upon meekness and humility as desirable qualities, especially if one is to be a truly religious person. One should be careful to note, however, that meekness and humility are qualities which are understood to exhibit strength, not weakness; integrity, not deceit; and to engender obedience to God rather than call attention to one's personal religiosity. Such qualities are still of value and are as necessary now as they were in Zephaniah's day.

NAHUM

The prophet Nahum did not deliver oracles against his own country; at least none is preserved. His teachings concern the nation Assyria. As one recalls, Assyria had been a major world power notorious for her brutality and atrocities; it was Assyria which had destroyed Israel and deported most of its people. Neither had Judah escaped the devastating power of Assyria's wrath (the campaign of Sennacherib ca. 701 B.C.).

The rise of Babylonia, however, coupled with internal weakness and decay, brought the great nation of Assyria to a sharp decline. By 625 B.C. it had become rather clear that Assyria's days were numbered. To that potential scene of destruction Nahum uttered his prophecy against Assyria. The date of the prophet is not certain, but most interpreters place him either around 625 B.C. or 612 B.C. The latter date is more likely.

The book seems to have been composed from two separate blocks of material. The first, found in chapter 1, was originally an acrostic poem (a poem in which each succeeding line began with successive letters of the Hebrew alphabet). The poem, however, as preserved, stops with the Hebrew letter "L." Was there another half of the poem? No clear answer is available. There are some scholars who believe that this poem was originally used in a formal cultic liturgy as part of the worship ritual.

The second section of the book is composed of numerous poems describing the fall of Nineveh and the unmitigated joy which Nahum and many others experienced at the thought that this wicked and vicious nation was finally being destroyed.

Study Outline for the Book of Nahum

   I. Yahweh's Judgment on the Wicked Nation: 1
   II. Descriptions of the Fall of Nineveh: 2–3

The opening verses of Nahum's proclamation depict Yahweh's just and righteous nature and the certain response which he makes to wickedness. Included also in chapter 1 are descriptions of the evils of the wicked nation against which Yahweh was about to move. Nahum spoke not only for God's people in Judah but also for other peoples of the world in expressing relief and even joy that judgment was coming to the Assyrians.

Chapters 2 and 3 describe in sometimes vivid detail the horrors of a people overrun by war. There are also various allusions to the Assyrians and their beliefs. For example, there is mention of lions and cubs (2:11-13). The patron goddess of Assyria was Ishtar, a war goddess frequently depicted riding on a lion. Thus the lion was quite frequently used as a symbol for Assyria. Ishtar was also considered a lustful goddess, an idea which may be reflected in 3:4.

The most telling of all the oracles was selected by the final redactors of the collection to conclude the prophecies of Nahum:

> Your shepherds are asleep,
>   O king of Assyria;
>   your nobles slumber.
> Your people are scattered on the mountains
>   with none to gather them.
> There is no assuaging your hurt,
>   your wound is grievous.
> All who hear the news of you
>   clap their hands over you.
> For upon whom has not come
>   your unceasing evil?
>
> —3:18-19

There are some persons who question whether such a book should be included in the sacred Scriptures. After all, such unmitigated rejoicing at the brutal destruction of a people seems to be something less than a "divine" reaction. Is what appears to be utter hatred worthy of "religious" people?

Such questions are not illegitimate, but they miss the point of the book's teaching. The point is that God does judge the evil of this world; his justice may seem to the human mind slow in its appearance, but his justice surely does come. Nations and peoples who cruelly, mercilessly, and capriciously inflict un-thinkable atrocities and sufferings upon others surely will come under God's righteous judgment. This book's teaching seems to declare without equivocation that there is a place for "righteous indignation," an abhorrence of such evil deeds no matter who perpetrates them. If evil is allowed to run rampant, by its very nature it will destroy even the last vestiges of good, truth, and justice. The idea that "might makes right" is not a biblical teaching. If God is a God of justice and righteousness, there is a place for judgment on those who defy his laws and cause horrible suffering. If not, what hope do we have?

There are numerous illustrations from the past which demonstrate this point. How many can the reader recall?

HABAKKUK

Dating the prophet Habakkuk is difficult since so little is known about this interesting character. Most scholars date Habakkuk in the late seventh century B.C., but other conjectures range all the way down to the time of Alexander the Great (ca. 330 B.C.). Very little concrete evidence is gained from the text itself, but there is a reference to the "Chaldeans" (the Babylonians), which gives more weight to the late seventh century or even early sixth century B.C.

One of the more interesting interpretative questions of this book involves the identity of those who were about to be destroyed by the Chaldeans. Some have identified these as the Assyrians. If this is true, the prophet Habakkuk would be dated about 626–612 B.C. and would have been a contemporary of Nahum both in terms of time and prophetic content. Since Habakkuk seems to be very puzzled by the events about to transpire and understands the conquered to have been less wicked than the Babylonians, it is much more probable that the people of Judah were intended as the victims here. The date of Habakkuk's prophecies, then, should be understood to have been delivered around 605–600 B.C., during the latter years of Jehoiakim's reign.

Another problem centers in the question of the book's original content. There is some evidence that chapters 1 and 2 may have existed for a period of time without chapter 3. In the collection of scrolls from the Dead Sea there is a text of Habakkuk which consists only of chapters 1 and 2, evidence that in some circles these two chapters may originally have existed by themselves.

Chapter 3 has its own superscription and seems to be a cultic hymn. Chapters 1 and 2 also reflect a cultic setting, however; some scholars suggest that these constituted a cultic liturgy. Since the first two chapters are similar in content and religious teaching to the third, it is not surprising to find that these were ultimately joined together into one literary unit. The genuine oracles of Habakkuk are probably to be found only in chapters 1 and 2, however.

Study Outline for the Book of Habakkuk

I. Dialogue Between Habakkuk and God: 1–2

II. Prayer-Hymn: 3

Habakkuk, like most of the preexilic prophets, believed that the people of Judah had broken God's covenant and were justly deserving of punishment. His perception of the world events of that time led him to understand that the Babylonians had been designated by God to deliver the judgment. This prophet, however, was somewhat more reflective in that he wished to understand why God would allow an admittedly evil nation to be overrun by one even more evil. His question involves the age-old problem of *theodicy*, the justice (or fairness) of God. (In this type of thinking Habakkuk is a forerunner of the speculative wisdom thinkers of the postexilic period who began to struggle specifically with theodicy as well as meaning and purpose in life.)

Having described the swift and brutal forces of the Chaldeans, Habakkuk asked his question:

> Thou who art of purer eyes than to behold evil
>   and canst not look on wrong,
> why dost thou look on faithless men,
>   and art silent when the wicked swallows up
>   the man more righteous than he?
>   —1:13

He then stationed himself in a tower to await an answer from Yahweh. The response finally came: "The righteous person shall live by his faithfulness" (2:4*b* paraphrase). This is almost the same answer the later wisdom thinkers espoused, one not always acceptable to or understood by human reasoning.

The prophet believed (in spite of not receiving a specific answer to his searching question) that God's will and justice gave ultimate meaning to the world's ongoing story, even when human beings did not understand. The hymn in chapter 3, though probably not part of Habakkuk's teaching, certainly reflects this message very pointedly:

> Though the fig tree do not blossom,
>   nor fruit be on the vines,
> the produce of the olive fail
>   and the fields yield no food,
> the flock be cut off from the fold
>   and there be no herd in the stalls,
> yet I will rejoice in the LORD,
>   I will joy in the God of my salvation.
>   —3:17-18

Persons today can always find injustices in life which seem arbitrary and undeserved. Why do these things happen? Why would God allow them to occur? There seem to be no more concrete solutions to these questions now than in the days of Habakkuk. The answer is the same: the truly righteous person will live in the confidence that God can and will make some sense out of this nonsense we call life.

JEREMIAH

Of all the prophets Jeremiah is the most "human." Perhaps this is a result of the fact that more is known about his life than any of the others or perhaps because he simply was more open with his personal feelings. He was a member of a priestly family in Anathoth, a village to the north of Jerusalem in the old area of Benjamin. Most scholars date the beginning of Jeremiah's prophetic ministry in the year 626 B.C., a date derived from the superscription to the book (1:1-3). There are, however, very few if any oracles which can really be dated earlier than about 609–605 B.C. The question arises, then: why was there such a long period with no prophetic message from Jeremiah? Some interpreters argue that this long silent period resulted from the fact that Jeremiah approved of Josiah's reform movement (which began ca. 621 B.C.), and, therefore, no oracles were really appropriate at that time.

There are other scholars, a minority at the present time, who interpret this long period without prophetic word in another way. They argue that Jeremiah understood his call to have been from his mother's womb (1:5) and that the year 626 was in reality the year of his birth. His ministry then did not begin until around 609–605 B.C., after Jehoiakim had become king and the reform movement had evaporated. Such an understanding also explains why Jeremiah always refers to Josiah as a figure of the past. Whatever date one accepts for the formal beginning of Jeremiah's ministry, there is no debate as to the fact that the bulk of his preaching took place during the reigns of Jehoiakim and Zedekiah (609–586 B.C.).

The book itself appears to have been edited in the form in which it presently exists through a rather long and complicated process, unfortunately unrecoverable now. Several collections of material dealing with Jeremiah and his teaching were used in the compilation of the book. The place to begin a study of the process lies in chapter 36 of the book. This chapter tells of an incident in Jeremiah's life when he called in his friend and scribe, Baruch, and dictated to him some of the oracles he had delivered against Judah. These were written on a scroll which Baruch took to the temple to read aloud. Certain of the nobles, having heard the reading, took the scroll to King Jehoiakim to read it to him. After hearing the contents, Jehoiakim cut the scroll into small pieces and burned them; whereupon Jeremiah dictated another collection or oracles, even enlarging the first scroll. Most scholars believe that some, if not most, of chapters 1–25 of the present book probably can be traced to that second scroll dictated by Jeremiah.

A second collection contains biographical data relating incidents in the life of the prophet. These chapters, 26–29 and 34–45, are basically prose accounts and show definite signs of having been redacted by the Deuteronomic editors (a group responsible for the final writing and editing of Deuteronomy, Joshua, Judges, First and Second Samuel, First and Second Kings). Some interpreters believe that Baruch originally preserved these traditional narratives about Jeremiah.

In addition, the book includes a series of oracles against foreign nations (chapters 46–51). Interestingly enough, these chapters are found following 25:13a in the Greek translation of the Old Testament (called the Septuagint, translated around 200–100

B.C.). This curious phenomenon raises questions about how this book (and perhaps others) reached its final form. The Greek translation uses the typical order of the larger prophetic books: oracles against the nation, oracles against foreign nations, hope passages, and historical data. The Hebrew text, however, has an altered arrangement, with the oracles against foreign nations having been moved to the end of the book. It is also interesting to note here that the Greek text of Jeremiah is about one-eighth shorter than the Hebrew text.

Another block of material is found in chapters 30–33. These chapters are frequently called the "Book of Consolation," a collection of hope and restoration passages. Some interpreters divide them into two segments, 30–31 and 32–33, but most likely they had already been placed together by the time the final editing process began.

It is possible to locate smaller and shorter collections within larger ones. The most famous of these consists of a series of personal laments uttered by Jeremiah, usually labeled the "confessions." The passages are found in 11:18–12:6; 15:10-21; 17:12(14)-18; 18:18-23; and 20:7-18. Much can be learned about Jeremiah's lonely and tragic life from these laments, and it is because of their content that Jeremiah is quite frequently known as the "weeping" prophet.

Study Outline for the Book of Jeremiah

   I. Oracles Against Judah: 1:1–25:14
  II. Oracles Against Foreign Nations: 25:15-38; 46–51
 III. Biographical Stories of Jeremiah's Life: 26–29; 34–45
 IV. Oracles of Restoration: 30–33
  V. Historical Appendix: 52

Oracles Against Judah

The ministry of Jeremiah probably began with his being told by Yahweh to go and deliver a message at the temple. How important an event this was may be surmised by the fact that the story appears in two places in the book, chapters 7 and 26. At this time the people had come to place such confidence in the temple that they were absolutely certain that as long as the temple was in Jerusalem no harm could come to them. Jeremiah's message was to shatter the tranquility of such misguided thinking, and the message proved to be quite startling to the people and their leaders. Just how much antagonism was generated can be seen in the fact that Jeremiah almost lost his life over this "sermon" (chapter 26). Someone recalled, however, that Micah had spoken equally harsh words about a century earlier (Micah 3:12); this saved Jeremiah from the wrath of the leaders for the moment. Another prophet, named Uriah, who prophesied against Jerusalem in this same period was executed by Jehoiakim himself (26:20-23)! The threat to Jeremiah's life, therefore, was not an empty one.

Because of his understanding of God, God's will, and God's requirements, Jeremiah always had the role of an adversary against the people of Judah, especially their leaders. Jeremiah came to learn very early that the majority of the people did not "know" the laws and requirements of Yahweh. Their hearts were sinful, even to the point of being incapable of doing good. Jeremiah understood, however, that these were not the key persons in reformation; they could follow but not lead. So, when he turned to the leaders in an attempt to find some point at which repentance could be appreciated and implemented, he found that the leaders were just as bad as, if not worse than, the people (5:1-5).

Jeremiah obviously carried on a continuous battle with the religious as well as political leadership of the country. He told Jehoiakim that his funeral would be like that of a dead jackass (22:18-19) and accused the religious leaders of using their revered status for personal gain (23:23-32). The prophets and priests had reached a very sad state when their offices were filled by persons who had no real understanding of what religion was all about.

In spite of Jeremiah's warnings the nation continued on its wayward path, and in 597 B.C. the Babylonians captured Jerusalem. Surprisingly enough, they did not destroy the city or the temple even though they did carry away a number of political and religious leaders into exile. Perhaps one reason for leniency was the death of Jehoiakim (who had actually led the rebellion) shortly before the city was captured. Another evidence of leniency was demonstrated when the Babylonians placed a person of Davidic descent (Zedekiah) on the throne. To be sure, Zedekiah was selected to be a vassal of Babylonia, but considering what had happened to Israel previously, these exactions were mild indeed.

In the interim between the first deportation in 597 B.C. and the destruction of Jerusalem in 586 B.C., Jeremiah's life was especially in danger. Twice he was thrown into an empty cistern to die. His preaching during this time was especially pointed. He believed that it was Yahweh's will to yield to the Babylonians and urged the people to submit to that yoke (chapter 27). The attitude and behavior of the people remaining in Judah were extremely bad, so bad that Jeremiah became convinced that any hope for the future of the nation lay with the exiles in Babylon. This teaching is clearly presented in the famous "vision" of the two baskets of figs, one very good and one very bad. The good figs were those in Babylon; the bad, those left in Judah (chapter 24). Hope for any restoration would have to come from the people in exile.

One very interesting incident occurred during the second siege of Jerusalem (chapter 34). The Babylonians had surrounded the city and cut it off from the outside world. The law required that any persons who owned slaves must feed and clothe them, no matter what the circumstances. In order to circumvent this obligation the owners declared the slaves to be "free." Shortly thereafter, when the Babylonians lifted the siege momentarily to take care of an Egyptian matter, the order freeing the slaves was rescinded. Jeremiah was convinced that such hypocrisy must be punished.

During his ministry Jeremiah performed numerous prophetic signs, several of which are quite well known. Jeremiah broke a pottery flask to demonstrate that Yahweh was about to destroy the nation (chapter 19). He also hid a loincloth along a body of water to show that as the loincloth was ruined by the water, so, too, was the nation of Judah being corrupted with idolatrous actions and attitudes (chapter 13). There were the incidents with the yokes (chapters 27–28) and his refusal to marry (an unthinkable course of action in those days) to show that in the coming judgment children and wives would suffer greatly. In addition to these, Jeremiah performed several other signs (chapters 35, 43, and 51).

Hope Passages

There is much debate concerning the collection of restoration and hope passages in the book of Jeremiah. Many interpreters believe that all these passages (chapters 30–33) were postexilic additions to Jeremiah's original teachings. Not all scholars agree with this assessment, however. It seems clear that the historical situation during Jeremiah's ministry probably precipitated a change in the preexilic prophetic message of doom. During Jeremiah's ministry the preexilic threats of destruction were actualized, thereby encouraging the prophet to begin to rethink what God's will and purpose might be now that the judgment had occurred.

From a careful reading of Jeremiah's authentic oracles one finds very clear evidence that the prophet understood his ministry to be not only one of proclaiming doom but also one of "building and planting" (1:10). It appears that he definitely believed in some sort of restoration in the land after a period of exile (chapters 24, 25, 29). To solidify this idea in the minds of the people, Jeremiah performed another of his famous signs. He bought a piece of property to assure the people of Judah that at some future time fields could be bought and sold again, a sign that the people would be restored in the land and that a certain measure of stability would also return (chapter 32).

With these incidents and background in mind it is not an unlikely conclusion that the oracles of hope in chapters 30–31 are genuinely from Jeremiah himself. They may have been slightly altered by the editors and redactors, but essentially they reflect Jeremiah's own religious understandings. The most famous of these teachings is contained in the "new covenant" passage, 31:31-34. The latter part of these verses, though not always identified as such, are mainly poetic in nature. Therefore, they are set as poetry here:

> "Behold, the days are coming, says the LORD, when I will make a new covenant with the house of Israel and the house of Judah, not like the covenant which I made with their fathers when I took them by the hand to bring them out of the land of Egypt, my covenant which they broke, though I was their husband, says the LORD. But this is the covenant which I will make with the house of Israel after those days, says the LORD:

I will put my law within them,
   and I will write it upon their hearts;
and I will be their God,
and they shall be my people.

And no longer shall each man teach his neighbor
   and each his brother, saying,
'Know the LORD,'
for they shall all know me,
from the least of them to the greatest, says the LORD;
for I will forgive their iniquity,
and I will remember their sin no more."

There are numerous ideas in this oracle which are character-
istic of Jeremiah's teaching. Central is the idea of a broken
covenant followed by a restoration of the covenant relationship
with a new law written on the hearts of the people. *All* would
be in the proper relationship with Yahweh because God would
have forgiven the sins of the people. All these elements were
indeed genuine concerns and staples of Jeremiah's understanding of Yahweh and his relationship with the people of Judah.
There could and would be a restoration, not because the people
deserved it but because God still had some plan and purpose
for the people. It was becoming clearer, however, that the purposes of God for these people were much broader and more
grandiose than they had ever understood, much less accepted.

The Tragedy of Jeremiah's Life

Jeremiah was looked upon as a traitor by his own people,
some of whom schemed and attempted to have the prophet
killed. Yet, since he understood the hypocrisy of the people and
the nature of God, his message was one of realism in the midst
of those troubled times. If the leaders had listened to Jeremiah,
the nation could have been spared most, though not all, of its
troubles, especially the harsh military conquest. They never
learned, however, and even after the second defeat (586 B.C.)
there were some who still plotted against Babylonia. The gov-
ernor Gedaliah, who had been placed in that capacity by Nebuchadnezzar, was the victim of a murder plot, which Jeremiah
condemned. After the deed had been completed, the group
perpetrating the revolt fled to Egypt, forcing Jeremiah to accom-
pany them (chapters 40–44). Tradition has it that Jeremiah was

stoned to death by these people in the land of Egypt. Although he had always spoken the truth, seen his warnings come to pass, and been vindicated by those occurrences, Jeremiah was never appreciated or heeded by his fellow countrymen. That kind of situation would be enough to cause one to become known as a "weeping" prophet.!

There have always been those persons of sensitive nature and keen insight who have the uncanny ability to read correctly the "signs of the times," to understand exactly where certain actions will lead and what the consequences of those actions will be. Unfortunately, these people also usually have the curse of Cassandra, that mythical woman who possessed the ability to see the future but was cursed by the fact that no one ever believed her. Jeremiah was one such person. He was able to read the moral climate of the people and possessed the insight to relate that understanding to contemporary world or local events. There are those in recent history who have had such gifts, and there are those presently who also have this unique ability. It is hoped that contemporary persons will be more open to their insights than the people of Jeremiah's time were to his words.

Probably the most impressive personal quality of Jeremiah was his courage. This man endured great hardship and suffering for his commitment to the prophetic call. His loyalty to Judah's people and leaders, even though they scorned his wisdom, remains as a great challenge to religious people of every generation. It is indeed a unique individual who can shift his teaching appropriately from doom to hope as historical situations are altered. Are there any Jeremiahs today who can speak to our present situation? And if there are, shall we be willing to listen?

EZEKIEL

The prophet Ezekiel was among those carried into Babylonian exile in 597 B.C., during the first deportation. His call to be a prophet came around 593 B.C. (1:1-3) in Babylon during a thunderstorm! On this occasion he saw the throne-chariot of Yahweh in the midst of the air. At least two major religious ideas are incorporated into this account. First, there is the understanding that Yahweh had not been "destroyed" by the defeat of the nation and the deportation of the people. In those days, quite frequently it was assumed that when a nation or people were destroyed and deported, the god of that nation no longer existed. Not so with the God of the Hebrew people—Yahweh transcended such ideas. The nation owed its existence to Yahweh, not Yahweh to the nation. The second, related idea plainly emphasized that Yahweh was present in Babylon just as he had been in Judah. His presence with the people was not diminished because of the different geographical locale. Again, many persons in that time understood a god's power and presence to be limited to a particular place, but Yahweh was not so limited.

At the time of his call Ezekiel was thirty years old. From the biblical accounts one learns that he was first a priest, which explains why there is such an emphasis in his teaching on proper form and order in worship. In fact, Ezekiel located one of the chief sins of the people in their failure to worship properly. He believed that the future for the people of God centered in a new community, restored in Judah and revolving around proper worship in a new temple in Jerusalem.

One of the major problems related to Ezekiel's prophetic ministry concerns exactly where he performed his tasks. The reader of the book is told that Ezekiel was in Babylon, but in several places the setting for the oracles is Judah, especially Jerusalem. Questions as well as theories abound at this point. Did Ezekiel carry on a ministry in both places? Was he already a prophet before he left Judah? Have the accounts of two or more prophets been telescoped together into one figure? Or was the actual *ministry* of Ezekiel carried out in Babylon while he received frequent reports of how things were going back in Judah? This latter seems most likely, especially when one recalls that the early period of Ezekiel's work was carried out during that horrible interval between the first deportation in 597 B.C. and the second, more destructive one in 586 B.C. From the Book of Jeremiah one learns that evil practices continued in Judah during this interim, and also that communication was evidently very open between Judah and Babylonia.

The Book of Ezekiel, upon first examination, appears to be a neatly structured and well-ordered collection of oracles from the life of the prophet. Many of the oracles are dated, the last from around 571 B.C., as if the prophet may have originally written down the oracles now contained in the book. However, various scholars have detected in the book what appears to be carefuly constructed redaction or editing which points to later compilers rather than Ezekiel himself for the essential structure of the book. Some scholars even detect oracles from as early as the time of Manasseh (ca. 650 B.C.) to the late postexilic period (ca. 230 B.C.).

These conjectures are probably much too speculative; most of the contents of the book probably belong to Ezekiel even though edited by later hands. The fact that there is such diversity of thought in Ezekiel's prophecies is a result of the fact that he bridged the time span between the preexilic period and the postexilic, being technically an exilic prophet. It is not surprising, therefore, to find in his teachings both oracles of doom and judgment and oracles of restoration. Ezekiel's ministry was understood by him to be that of a "watchman" whose duty was to warn people of dangers even if they did not respond to that warning.

One of the major concerns in dealing with Ezekiel's life and work centers in the person of the prophet. It is obvious to the careful reader of the book that this man was rather unusual, to say the least. In fact, his behavior was downright bizarre. Some have attempted to analyze Ezekiel from the scriptural reports and have found him to be psychologically deranged. This conclusion, however, is somewhat unfair because we do not possess a full account of the man and his ministry. We do know, however, that his culture was quite different from ours and that many of the bizarre actions Ezekiel performed were prophetic signs. Having said all these things in Ezekiel's behalf, one is nevertheless still somewhat puzzled by this *unusual* person.

It is interesting that the favorite term for Ezekiel in the book itself is "son of man." This phrase occurs over ninety times, and in Hebrew it carries the meaning of "man" usually with the nuance of finiteness or weakness. Ezekiel understood Yahweh to be majestic and exalted, high above human thought or comprehension, and this exalted view of God may have been a factor in his understanding of himself as a mere mortal, small and insignificant before such a powerful and awesome being.

Study Outline for the Book of Ezekiel

I. Oracles Against Judah and Jerusalem: 1–24
II. Oracles Against Foreign Nations: 25–32
III. Oracles of Restoration: 33–48
   A. Preparing for the return: 33–39
   B. Restoration of worship in the temple: 40–48

Oracles Against Judah and Jerusalem

The first major portion of the Book of Ezekiel contains oracles and signs against the nation of Judah, and it is because of these signs that many persons attribute a bizarre personality to the prophet. He took a brick, etched the outline of a city upon it and surrounded it with types of military siege equipment. Then he lay on his left side for 390 days and on his right for 40 days to portray the period of exile for Israel and Judah (4:1-8). He also cooked food over burning dung to illustrate the fact of exile (4:9-17). He shaved his head and divided the hair into thirds to demonstrate what would happen to the people of Jerusalem and Judah when the next destruction took place (chapter 5). He even felt commanded not to mourn the death of his wife as a sign that when Jerusalem was destroyed, the people would not have the opportunity to mourn the dead according to custom and feeling (chapter 24). These and other curious actions make Ezekiel a fascinating and peculiar figure.

One of the chief characteristics of Ezekiel's teaching centered in his understanding of Yahweh as a magnificent and majestic God, transcendent over all. This idea is encountered at the very outset in the call accounts. Ezekiel recognized from the beginning that Yahweh was not only in Judah but also present with the exiles in Babylon. Ezekiel had such an exalted understanding of God that it is not surprising to find that he depicted the major sin of the people as idolatry. Examples of how idolatrous the people in Judah had become are found in chapter 8. Here both the people and the religious leaders were worshiping the sun, different idols, and the fertility god of Babylonia, Tammuz. Yahweh's nature was such that he would not tolerate such effrontery under any circumstances; the nation in Judah would be destroyed. Ezekiel saw the "glory" of Yahweh (Yahweh himself) leave the temple, signifying that Yahweh had abandoned the people because of their sins (chapter 10; also chapter 22).

One of the most famous of Ezekiel's teachings illustrates Judah's punishment clearly. In chapter 23 there is an allegory of two sisters, Oholah and Oholibah. Oholah was a harlot, evil and faithless, who was punished because of her sins. Her sister, Oholibah, having seen all that had happened, did not learn any lesson from the fate of Oholah, but rather turned out to be even more evil. She, too, deserved and received punishment for her sins. Of course, Oholah represented Israel and Oholibah represented Judah.

Ezekiel's Ministry to the Exiles

Since Ezekiel ministered to the people in exile in addition to delivering oracles of doom to the nation of Judah, his book, therefore, has numerous teachings which reflect the problems of the exiles. One of the most important is found in chapter 18, which deals with the complaint of the exiles that they were suffering unfairly for the sins of their parents. Comprehension of Ezekiel's teaching here is important not only to understand the prophet's response to the exiles but also to correct earlier interpreters' misunderstandings of the chapter.

A popular approach to the interpretation of the Old Testament writings by scholars of the late nineteenth and early twentieth century suggested that religious ideas evolved from a lower to a higher level. One concept was that earlier forms of religion concentrated on the group while the later, more developed form centered in individuals. In the discussion of biblical religion on this issue, chapter 18 of Ezekiel (and to a lesser degree, Jeremiah 31:31-34) held a prominent place, for the teaching in this chapter was viewed as the turning point in the development of Hebrew religious thought. Prior to this time, it was argued, the individual had been considered as only a part of the larger and more important group; however, with this teaching of Ezekiel on the importance of each individual, the individual had broken free of the older, more primitive restrictions to stand alone in relationship to God and life. The fact is, however, that neither Ezekiel 18 nor Jeremiah 31:31-34 taught full-scale individualism. One recalls that the Jeremiah passage concentrated on the restoration of the nation, surely a corporate understanding. The Ezekiel passage deserves more careful consideration.

The Hebrew people in Babylon were quoting an old proverb to lament their fate, "The fathers have eaten sour grapes, and the children's teeth are set on edge" (18:2b). It is interesting to note that Ezekiel did not dispute the point that the people were in exile because of the sins of generations past. In the light of the "corporate personality" concept so strong in those times, there was no need to refute that statement. Since all the generations—past, present, and future—were supposedly incorporated in the group presently living, the ancient Hebrews did not really separate people into totally individual and separate entities.

The answer Ezekiel gave to these people did tend to be more individualistic than some earlier teachings, but the emphasis was still on the group. In chapter 18 Ezekiel spoke primarily to the individual who was found in a particular setting, in fact *any* setting. The idea was that, in spite of where one was or how one got into that situation, one could still be loyal to Yahweh and keep Yahweh's commands. If so, that person would live and have a good life. If not, that person would be destroyed for not being obedient to God's requirements. The clear implication was that the people were expected to repent and remain faithful to God no matter what their circumstances. If they did, God would bless them and continue their existence as a people. Ezekiel did not speak for individualism *per se*, however, for his vision of the future centered in a restored *community* in Jerusalem.

Oracles of Restoration

Since Ezekiel, even more so than Jeremiah, was a transition prophet, there are numerous oracles of hope for restoration for the people, as well as predictions of doom, to be found among his teachings. As already indicated, the basic hope was for a restoration of the people in the land of Judah. In the light of such an understanding, Ezekiel, along with several other prophets (especially Jeremiah 30–31), began to speak about a reunion between Israel and Judah. The question arises as to how such an idea may have developed and what exactly it meant—especially in the light of the fact that the northern Israelites had been settled in other lands and had long since been assimilated both culturally and physically into their new societies. Further, the settlement of foreign peoples in Israel by the Assyrians in order to repopulate that area (beginning about 721 B.C.) meant that the people of Judah no longer considered any of those people as part of the people of God. The population of old Israel was now racially mixed and, therefore, unclean. Yet some prophets did speak of reuniting Israel and Judah. What did that signify to them?

In all probability this idea began to arise during the reign of Josiah, who had been able to expand the territory of Judah because the Assyrians were under heavy attack from the Babylonians and could not control Palestine as they had done previously. Josiah at that time was able to exercise some control over part of what had formerly been the Northern Kingdom. It was probably this historical episode that gave rise to a political hope that the people of God would again control a kingdom as large and strong as that of David and Solomon. This hope, however, was postulated, not on a return of the northern peoples to Palestine, but rather on the expansion of southern power into the area formerly held during the united monarchy. Ezekiel believed this could occur, and he looked forward to a new David who would care for the people as a shepherd cares for his flock. Interestingly, this new David was not called a king but a "prince" (34:24).

The restoration of the people in Judah is presented in one of Ezekiel's most famous visions (chapter 37). He saw a great valley full of very dry bones, disconnected one from another. When the Spirit of God moved upon the bones, they were joined together, covered with flesh, and lived again. Here Ezekiel's understanding of the restoration of the nation is made clearly and pointedly. One must remember that this vision was not of the resurrection of individuals but the resurrection and restoration of the nation. This restoration was to be made possible by God's destruction of the enemies of his people. These enemies were depicted in chapter 38 under the titles "Gog" and "Magog."

For some reason these names—Gog and Magog—have held a peculiar fascination for certain persons, and fantastic theories have been proposed for their identification. The precise translation of the terms is not certain; the phrase could mean "Gog *and* Magog," or "Gog *from* Magog," or perhaps "Gog *even* Magog." The origin of the names is not certain, but it is obvious from their use in context that they refer to Babylonia. When that nation was destroyed, the people of God in Babylon would be allowed to return home. That was to be a great time, so great that Ezekiel "renamed" Jerusalem "Yahweh Is There" (see 48:35b). God and the people would be together in a new and special relationship. That was Ezekiel's hope.

Ezekiel, like Jeremiah, believed that this hope would be established and actualized through a new covenant between the people and God. Such a situation could only be accomplished, however, by giving the people a new heart, a heart made of flesh to replace their old heart of stone (36:26). True to his priestly background, Ezekiel understood this entire process to be centered in a ritual cleansing whereby the people would be made ceremonially and religiously clean once again.

The new community which he envisioned was to be a theocratic state, one focused on religious and cultic affairs revolving around the role of the priests located in the new temple. The description of this situation is elaborately given in chapters 40–48. Ezekiel believed that when the new temple was completed and all the cultic articles were in place, the glory of Yahweh would again enter the temple (see chapter 10 where the glory left the old temple). To illustrate his point, the prophet, in truly poetic fashion, depicts a river flowing from the temple through the land making it alive again. The power of this new force was to be so great that it would even make the Dead Sea come to life!

The teaching of Ezekiel is in many respects quite similar to that of Jeremiah (new covenant, sin residing in the corruption of the heart, and restoration after punishment); therefore modern applications of those ideas would remain the same. There are several other ideas emphasized by Ezekiel, however, which persons today could very well incorporate beneficially into their lives. His concept of God as majestic, even awe inspiring, depicts the power and might inherent in the God of the Scriptures. His emphasis upon God's presence with his people wherever they may be and in whatever circumstances is a concept which we need to regain in today's complicated and complex world. And finally, the idea that God's people are to live together, centering their lives in the proper worship of God, has much merit as well. One should not interpret Ezekiel, however, as someone who advocates only proper form and ritual. His emphasis upon a new heart of flesh exonerates him from such a charge. Yet there may be some truth in the understanding that a new life (or any life for that matter) which is acceptable to God must revolve around the proper worship of God and the keeping of God's laws. There is a delicate balance between becoming too preoccupied with external form and understanding God's requirements as only those ideas and styles which speak "to us." Correctly understood, Ezekiel attempts to establish a balance between the two areas, understanding each as important to a life which can be seen as truly religious.

ISAIAH 40–55

It is an accepted tenet of human logic that anything said or written presupposes some sort of specific historical setting, and if the interpreter can discover that setting, the meaning of the statement(s) will be much easier to understand. Such is the case with chapters 40–55 of the Book of Isaiah. Since 1892, with the work of the German scholar Bernhard Duhm, vigorous and commanding arguments have been accepted by most Old Testament scholars for separating chapters 40–66 from the eighth-century prophet whose teachings and biographical data are basically included in chapters 1–39. Isaiah of eighth-century Jerusalem could not possibly have been the same person who was in exile in Babylon around 550–540 B.C., speaking to the exiles and presenting to them the good news that Yahweh was about to allow them to return to Judah.

In fact, chapters 40–66 are usually divided into two sections, chapters 40–55 set within the Babylonian exile and chapters 56–66 (which will be discussed later) set within the restored community in Palestine. The question often asked concerns why the ancients would have collected the teachings of several different prophets from several different historical eras into the same book. Numerous answers could be given, but the most likely conclusion is that these teachings came from someone who was a part of the circle of persons preserving and transmitting the materials from Isaiah of eighth-century Jerusalem. If this were the case, these persons would have thought nothing wrong with placing all those oracles together. Their concepts of literary separateness and individual authorship were simply not the same as ours, and for us to impose our understandings onto their works is misleading at best.

Thus, chapters 40–66 should be recognized as having originated from a different person or persons than Isaiah 1–39. There are persons in modern times who feel that such analysis of the biblical material strips it of its inspired character. No such judgment is either necessary or warranted, however, for the recognition of a collection of works as having been situated in a given historical period says nothing about the inspiration of the material. That judgment was left to the community of God's people to determine, and it still is. (This is discussed more fully under "Problem Aspects of Isaiah.")

The prophet whose teachings are incorporated in Isaiah 40–55 is usually referred to as Second Isaiah or Deutero-Isaiah. His message was one of hope: God was about to lead the people in a new Exodus so that they might be reestablished in Judah. In the process, this prophet emphasized the greatness of Yahweh, ridiculing the gods of Babylon. It was during this period and in this setting that the major emphasis on Yahweh as the creator God began to be made in Israelite religious development. This was a result of the fact that the Babylonian religion made much of their god, Marduk, and his role in the creation of the universe. To counter this, the exiles developed a strong understanding of Yahweh as the Creator. (The creation account found in Genesis 1:1–2:3 may have originated about this same time.)

Directly related to this emphasis on the creative aspect of God's activity came the realization among the leaders of Hebrew religious thinking that not only was Yahweh the greatest of the gods, to be worshiped by the Hebrew people to the exclusion of all other gods, but Yahweh was the *only* God. This idea had been a long time in developing. To be sure, Yahweh had been understood as the only God the Hebrews could worship, but there was no real denial of the existence of other gods. Such an idea, the worship of one god without denying the existence of others, is called *henotheism*. With the teachings of Deutero-Isaiah, however, there was no longer any doubt about the worship of Yahweh; one worshiped Yahweh or no god at all because there was no god other than Yahweh. The henotheism of Israel's early days had now become a strict *monotheism*.

There is at least one other very complicated problem to be dealt with in a study of these prophetic teachings. Again Bernhard Duhm is the scholar whose name is connected with the beginning of this discussion. Duhm argued that there are in Isaiah 40–55 four poetic sections which should be understood as separate from the other oracles and probably should be attributed to someone other than the prophet whose words are found in the remainder of the collection. These four passages are: 42:1-4; 49:1-6; 50:4-9; and 52:13–53:12. They are designated as the "Servant Songs."

Probably more ink has been used in debating the issues connected with the problem of the servant in these chapters than with any other portion of the Old Testament writings. Many questions are discussed: Who was the servant? Is the servant an individual or a group? What role was the servant to play? Are these passages by another prophet? Should they be understood separately from the context in which they are found? And these are only some of the major issues!

Scholars are divided today in their answers to these problems, and thus almost every one will vary somewhat in presenting solutions. Several observations may be made at this point, however. It is generally agreed that even if the servant songs existed separately, they do reflect the same style and vocabulary as the remainder of chapters 40–55. Further, as one studies the entire collection, it becomes rather clear that the figure of the servant is not limited only to the four songs. Finally, as one examines the passages relating to the figure of the servant, it becomes obvious that at some points the servant is an individual and at other points the servant represents a group. How does one make sense of this troublesome set of problems? More specific discussion will follow.

Study Outline for the Book of Isaiah 40–55

  I. Oracles of Hope for the Exiles in Babylon: 40–48

 II. Oracles of Restoration for the Nation: 49–55

The material in Isaiah 40–55 can be easily divided into two

separate sections, but there is a variety of subject matter and religious teachings within each division. The basic theme for the entire section (40–55) is that of the restoration of the Jewish people in the land of Judah. This hope for restoration was rooted in an understanding that Yahweh was their God, that he was great and majestic, yes, the *only* God.

> Thus says [Yahweh], the King of Israel, . . .
> "I am the first and I am the last,
>   besides me there is no god."
>
> —44:6

It was this God who was about to lead the people out of exile in Babylon in a new Exodus. The flowery, poetic style of the prophet was at its best when he described how the desert would blossom; the valleys would be filled in, the mountains leveled; and oases would spring up all along the way (40:3-4). The idea expressed indicated that instead of having to return to Judah by the longer circular route (north, west, then south), they would be able to go directly from Babylon west to Palestine through the desert and the mountains! One is reminded, however, that such ideas are poetic and should be understood as such.

The most controversial points of interpretation lie, as already indicated, with the problems surrounding the figure of the servant of Yahweh (the *'Ebed-Yahweh*). The conclusions one reaches with regard to these matters are to a great degree dependent on whether one understands the four servant passages to be written by a different person or by the same prophet as the remainder of 40–55. The position taken in this discussion is that these songs are so similar in style and content to the remainder of the oracles that they should be interpreted as having originated with the same person.

The Identity of a Servant

Having arrived at this conclusion, however, the interpreter is still left with many unanswerable questions, not the least of which concerns just who the servant was. Some argue for the servant's being an individual, and numerous suggestions have been made of that individual's identity: Moses, Jehoiachin, Jeremiah, a leprous teacher of the law, the prophet himself, to cite only a few conjectures. Or is the servant to be understood as a corporate figure, and, if so, what group is meant? Israel? Ideal Israel? A small group within Israel? And what is the background for the figure? Is it a priestly figure, a messianic figure, a kingly figure, or a prophetic figure? No unanimity of opinion has as yet evolved among the various Old Testament scholars, but after a careful study of the text certain ideas seem to be obvious.

The identity of the servant seems to be the people Israel. In those passages not included in the four special songs, this identification is plain: "But now hear, O Jacob my servant, Israel whom I have chosen!" (44:1; also 42:18-25; 43:8-10). In one of the songs (49:3) there is even a phrase which specifically designates the servant as Israel. The problem with this identification, according to some scholars, is that the phrase disrupts the poetic metre and is therefore viewed by them as a later understanding and interpretation written into the text. Such arguments are taken more seriously by some than by others; even if the phrase was a later addition, however, it may simply have been an editor's way of making the meaning precise.

Other problems persist, however. The servant was said to have had a mission to perform to Israel. How could Israel have performed a ministry to itself? This question does not appear to be so nettlesome if one remembers the Hebrew tendency to think basically in corporate terms. An individual could represent (even be) the group, or a small segment of the larger whole could be understood as the entire group itself. Since these people also understood the past and future generations to be included within the living group, it is not surprising to find passages which speak of past or present events affecting the entire group either in the present or in the future. With such an understanding Israel could have had a mission to Israel, and the servant could have been depicted as the entire group, a part of the larger unit, or even as an individual. In Isaiah 40-55 the servant was depicted as all of these!

The Function of the Servant

What was the primary function of the servant? From the texts in which the figure of the servant appears, one learns that the servant had a ministry to Israel, but more importantly the servant's task was to be directed toward the entire world. This task was to be a renewal of God's primary purpose when Abraham and his descendants were elected "to be God's special people." Election was not understood by the biblical writers as a position of privilege as much as it was a position of responsibility. The call to Abraham was centered in the task of making the "name" (i.e., the Person) of God known in all the world. Deutero-Isaiah, speaking to the exiles many centuries later, reiterated that same call, which had yet to be either fully understood or fully accepted by Israel. These people were to be restored so that they could resume what had been God's purpose for them from the time of Abraham. The servant passages make this point very clearly:

"It is too light a thing that you should be my servant
    to raise up the tribes of Jacob
    and to restore the preserved of Israel;
I will give you as a light to the nations,
    that my salvation may reach to the end of the earth."
                                                —49:6

Interestingly enough, the great prophet of the Exile believed (as had other prophets) that Yahweh could and did use other people and/or nations in accomplishing his purposes. In fact many modern persons are quite shocked upon learning that Deutero-Isaiah called the great Persian king, Cyrus, Yahweh's messiah (see 44:28 and 45:1)! Cyrus was the one selected by God to be the means whereby the people would be released and allowed to return to Judah.

The Concept of Vicarious Suffering

The most unusual of all the teachings of this prophet is incorporated in the last and most famous of the servant songs, 52:13–53:12. Here the concept of vicarious suffering is decisively introduced into the religious teaching of the Old Testament. Vicarious suffering means suffering which is experienced and endured by one not deserving of it, suffering which holds the possibility that somehow through the suffering others may be redeemed or their lives enhanced.

From what source the prophet derived this idea is not known precisely. He could have interpreted the destruction of the nation and the subsequent exile of the people as a form of vicarious suffering which would benefit the generations to come; or perhaps he modeled the concept after someone, possibly a religious figure from the exilic community who had suffered on behalf of the larger group. The religious teaching remains the same no matter where the idea originated. The concept suggests that an innocent person or persons, through undeserved suffering (not as a result of their sin) could be the means whereby other persons might have a better life. It was a very new idea set forth by this prophet and one which attempted to give an answer to one of the problems related to the fact of human misery.

It is interesting to note how long it took for this idea to surface in the development of Hebrew religious thought. This teaching was not popular at the time of the prophetic writing, and the dawning of the concept came only from the specific historical situation of the Exile. It is worth noting that this concept does not appear again in the Old Testament writings.

The entire collection of these marvelous oracles from the great prophet of the Exile was concluded with a challenge to the community to accept Yahweh's redemption, restoration, and purpose. The prophet ends with this description of the joy waiting to be experienced in the return of the people to their old land and their restoration within it.

> "For you shall go out in joy,
>   and be led in peace;
> and the mountains and the hills before you
>   shall break forth into singing,
>   and all the trees of the field shall clap their hands.
> Instead of the thorn shall come up the cypress;
>   instead of the brier shall come up the myrtle;
> and so it shall be to the LORD for a memorial,
>   for an everlasting sign which shall not be cut off."
>   —55:12-13

Problem Aspects of Isaiah

This portion (40–55) of the Book of Isaiah has been the center of much controversy for quite some time. Many contemporary persons do not understand why these oracles were incorporated into the ancient scroll of Isaiah if they were not genuine teachings of the Isaiah of the eighth century. For such persons the idea of a "second" Isaiah is exceedingly disturbing. The recognition that these chapters reflect a different time, place, and person should not really be disturbing, however. To recognize that these teachings come from a different historical setting only enables the serious student of the Bible to understand the text better.

The fact that these teachings originated in different places need not detract in any way from the inspiration of the passages, as some have argued. Surely God can and does inspire persons in every age to speak the appropriate word to his people in whatever circumstances. In fact it would have been very unusual if no prophetic voice had been heard during the period of the Exile. That this voice probably originated among those who had preserved and treasured the teachings of the eighth-century Isaiah and that these sayings were subsequently included in the large scroll emanating from that group should not really surprise or trouble us. It is well known that the standards of literary propriety accepted by persons in that time were not the same as those of the present era. Their standards should not be judged by our criteria. The final editors of the scroll of Isaiah, which stands first in the collection of the latter prophets, may very well have had a theological purpose in mind by arranging the book as they did, for the arrangement reflected the experience of the people for whom the book was originally prepared. The three segments representing the sin of the nation (1–39), the Exile and cleansing (40–55), and the restoration in the land (56–66) may have been so placed as to demonstrate graphically the history of the people of God and to illustrate how God related to them in each of these moments of their history.

A second major problem evolves for Christians when it becomes clear that the servant passages were not predictions of Jesus as many have often thought. In fact, these passages were not even considered messianic until the New Testament community interpreted Jesus' ministry in the light of Isaiah 52:13–53:12. The only messiah in Isaiah 40–55 is Cyrus, the Persian king! It is also clear that even if (as some argue) the prophet was "under inspiration" and speaking "more than he knew," the figure of the servant in Isaiah 40–55 does not fit precisely as a prediction which was literally fulfilled later. Many of the descriptions given for the servant cannot be applied to Jesus. For example, the servant was blind and deaf (42:19), had committed transgressions and sins (44:22), and was said to have had children (53:10)! Therefore, if someone wishes to understand the "servant" as having been fulfilled in the person of Jesus of Nazareth, the fulfillment must be on a level other than the literal, historical, predictive level. In fact, there is quite a bit of evidence that the early Christians interpreted Jesus' ministry as a special fulfillment of the servant motif, but not as literal prediction-fulfillment. After all, the important element in the religious teachings of the biblical books is the underlying truth for which the historical setting has only formed the "container." One must be very careful not to confuse the "container" with the content, for to do that would be to obscure and possibly lose the real truth contained in the Scripture. The fulfillment by Jesus of the servant teachings must come at the *essential* level, not at the *superficial* level. (See the discussion about the X level and the Y level in James M. Efird, *Jeremiah: Prophet Under Siege* [Valley Forge: Judson Press, 1979], pp. 15-16.)

The messages of hope for God's people, of God's purpose to make all nations know his law and justice, of the magnificent vision of Yahweh as Creator of all, and of the call for vicarious suffering make this prophet one of the most creative and influential of the prophetic voices.

CHAPTER 3

The Postexilic Prophets

The reader is encouraged at this point to reread the portion of the historical survey which deals with the postexilic era of Judean history (pp. 24-26). The primary points to keep in mind when studying the prophets of this period are that the times were very harsh for the people, who were attempting to reestablish themselves, and that very little specifically is known about the history of the people during those difficult days. Since the historical circumstances were so changed during these times, the prophetic message was somewhat mixed when compared to the preexilic proclamation of doom and the exilic hope for restoration. In the postexilic period the people needed to be challenged, chastened, and at times encouraged. The prophets attempted to deliver the appropriate message whenever it was needed.

There are many scholars who label the prophetic activity in the postexilic period as the time of decline or decay for this once marvelous movement. It would be less than fair, however, if that understanding were allowed to characterize the conclusion of the prophetic times. Certainly the prophetic voice was being heard less and less, and the prophetic ministry was becoming less and less a focal point in the lives of the people. But this circumstance was a result of the fact that the historical matrix which supplied the proper environment for the rise and continuation of the movement was no longer present. The prophets were not so much in decline (in the negative sense) as they were no longer the most appropriate medium to bring God's revelation to his people. The place of the prophets was being taken by other movements more suited to speak to the needs of the people at that particular moment of history. The postexilic period became the time for the flowering of the wisdom movement (shown in the books of Job, Ecclesiastes, and Proverbs). This was the time for the finalization of the traditons of the past into written documents which would speak not only of the past but to the people's present circumstances as well (the Torah, including Genesis through Deuteronomy; the Deuteronomic history, including Joshua through Kings; the work of the chronicler in Chronicles, Ezra, Nehemiah); and the time of the very popular apocalyptic movement which spoke directly to people who were powerless and were experiencing persecution (found especially in Daniel 7–12). The prophetic movement did come to an end, historically speaking, but its insights and teachings were to stand the tests of time because these committed prophets of God had shared their vision of Yahweh's power and person with courage and conviction, even though the people often refused to listen. In the providence of God these revelations were not lost but preserved by those who understood something of the importance of the messages.

The prophets of the postexilic times were also speaking to the people but in a different historical situation. Their messages, while not as exciting or striking as those of their more well-known and flamboyant predecessors, are no less valid. Each group contributed to the ongoing revelation of God.

HAGGAI

Deutero-Isaiah had painted a glowing poetic portrait of life in the restored community, but upon arriving in the land in about 538 B.C. the returnees found themselves in a very depressing situation. The land had been left alone for almost fifty years; there were no thriving settlements. Any portion of land which was of value had been possessed by other people not willing to relinquish their rights to it. The people who lived in the area of the old Northern Kingdom were considered unclean and impure by the newly returned exiles. The land was vulnerable to attack from almost any nation or people who happened to decide to take something from the defenseless Judeans.

It appears that shortly after the return, the people did lay the foundation for a new temple. Being preoccupied with simple survival, however, they neglected to complete that task. Politically Judah was a part of the Persian system of government and not a separate and distinct political state. This was something of a disappointment to the persons who had returned from exile and who had been led to believe that they would be part of a great new political entity which would arise among them shortly after their return. Unfortunately, these expectations did not transpire, and very difficult times faced them in their rebuilding process. Crop failures also may have added to their miseries. The grim realities of their situation caused the people great despair and disillusionment.

There came a moment, however, shortly after the return, when some saw a glimmer of hope for the restoration of the nation as a political entity. Upon the death of Cambyses II (Cyrus's son, ca. 521 B.C.) the Persian Empire experienced many internal problems. At that point some of the people in Judah felt that the time was right for the resurrection of the nation to its former greatness. The religious leaders believed that this could not be accomplished, however, apart from the rebuilding of the temple. If the temple were rebuilt, that would inaugurate the new age of greatness for the people of God. This hope was centered in a descendant of the Davidic line, a grandson of Jehoiachin named Zerubbabel.

Thus, from 520 to 515 B.C. there was a period of great activity accompanied by high hopes among the people in Judah. The turmoil which had occurred within the Persian government was brought under control, however, and the power of the Persian state was reasserted over all areas of the empire. When this happened, the hopes for a restoration of the nation in Judah were shattered. It was in this situation that the prophets Haggai and Zechariah exercised their ministries. Haggai especially centered his efforts on exhorting the people to rebuild the temple.

Study Outline for the Book of Haggai

I. Description of a Grim Situation Resulting from Neglect of the Temple: 1

II. Promises for a New Nation: 2

The message of Haggai was rather simple. The people were not prospering because they had failed to rebuild God's house, the temple. If they rebuilt the temple, their fortunes would change for the better. Haggai hoped for the restoration of the nation under the leadership of Zerubbabel, whom he thought would be a messiah. ". . . . I will take you, O Zerubbabel my servant, the son of Shealtiel, says the LORD, and make you like a signet ring; for I have chosen you, says the LORD of hosts" (2:23). It is interesting to note that shortly after the events depicted in Haggai and Zechariah, Zerubbabel disappeared from the scene and was heard from no more. Many scholars believe that once the internal problems of the Persian Empire had been settled and more attention was directed toward what was happening in the provinces, Zerubbabel was viewed as a potential threat to stability in the area and taken away. There is no concrete record of this, but many believe such must have occurred.

There are two basic teachings which one finds upon a close study of the material in the book of Haggai. The first one conforms to the old religious ideology found so frequently in the prophetic teachings usually known as the "Deuteronomic theology." This teaching was quite simple. It held that if a person was loyal to Yahweh and his commands, that person would be rewarded. On the other hand, if a person was not loyal to Yahweh and his commands, that person would be punished. Haggai basically understood God's relationship with the people in Judah in this light. They were not prospering because they had neglected Yahweh and Yahweh's affairs. If they altered that situation, good things would begin to happen for them. Haggai's teaching, however, seemed to emphasize the obligation to be loyal to God and keep his commands even when things were not going right. Quite frequently people in such situations adhered to doing things properly for a while, but if dramatic changes in fortune were not forthcoming almost immediately, they tended to become lax, assuming that things would never be right. Haggai seemed to be challenging the people to continue doing what was required even if results were delayed. (The fact that in life the positive results sometimes *never* come is wrestled with in the wisdom movement in the books of Job and Ecclesiastes.)

The second emphasis found in Haggai's teaching centered on the problem of "clean" and "unclean." These terms are primarily to be understood in the cultic sense; being clean enables one to be a full-scale member of the theocratic community, and being unclean excludes one from participating in the life of the community. Haggai emphasized the understanding that one could not become clean simply by coming into contact with something clean, but one could become unclean by coming into contact with something unclean. The people were therefore urged to consecrate themselves to the proper worship of God and the keeping of the precepts of that worship. By so doing, their lives would continue to be clean, and they would be the true people of God (see 2:1-19). It is interesting to note that Haggai predicted great rewards for the community centering in the temple: "The latter splendor of this house shall be greater than the former, says the LORD of hosts; and in this place I will give prosperity . . ." (2:9).

There are several principles in Haggai's teaching that are valid even for these times. His emphasis upon the responsibility to continue to do what is proper and required even when things are not going well is admirable indeed. Far too many persons believe that one's responsibility to do right is only valid as long as one's life is tranquil and pleasant. If situations arise, either short-term or long-term, in which one experiences difficulties, somehow one is relieved of the responsibility to do right. The teaching here is that one must continue to do right no matter what external circumstances may transpire.

The second idea of Haggai which holds some significance for persons today lies in his teaching about cleanness and uncleanness. While it is clear that Haggai is speaking in ritualistic terms, to the Hebrew mind there was a definite connection between ritual and reality. It may not, then, be too much to suggest that the teaching can be applicable even today though modern people do not usually recognize a direct connection between cultic purity and ethical purity. The principle here is plain. One can become "unclean" by contact with things unclean, but one cannot become "clean" merely by contact with things clean. Uncleanness by its nature is highly "contagious," but cleanliness must constantly be guarded, protected, and labored for. Evil can "rub off" on a person, but being good is a quality which requires constant and diligent effort.

ZECHARIAH 1–8

Zechariah, who was also a priest, was a contemporary of Haggai, serving in about 520–515 B.C. This prophet believed, as did Haggai, that God was going to usher in a new age for the people of Judah and that Zerubbabel was to have an important part in this great happening.

One of the most significant developments in the prophetic message of Zechariah was the tendency to portray his ideas in vision form. This does not mean, of course, that visions were not part of the revelatory process for the prophets in earlier times, but with Zechariah the visions became more graphic and bizarre, even more so than with Ezekiel! This tendency was to become a trend in the postexilic times, developing eventually into the wild visions of the apocalyptic movement. There is a genuine puzzle, however, in the interpretation of these visions. Scholars are divided in their discussions as to whether these visions were actually seen by the prophet or seer in some type of ecstatic trance or dream, or whether these visions were literary devices used by various persons to dramatize the message they wished to proclaim. Although there is no real consensus on this matter among interpreters, the interpretation of the vision is usually the same no matter which view one accepts as to its origin.

The historical context of the Book of Zechariah reflected in chapters 1–8 is that of the early postexilic era contemporary with Haggai. The last chapters, 9–14, reflect later historical periods and will be discussed within their appropriate time slots.

Study Outline for the Book of Zechariah 1–8

I. Introduction: 1:1-6
II. A Series of Night Visions: 1:7–6:8
    A. The four horsemen patroling the earth: 1:7-17
    B. The four horns and four smiths: 1:18-20
    C. The measuring of Jerusalem: 2:1-5
    D. The forgiveness of the priest: 3
    E. The lampstand and two olive trees: 4
    F. The flying scroll: 5:1-4
    G. The women taken to Babylon: 5:5-11
    H. The four chariots: 6:1-8
III. The Coronation of Joshua (Zerubbabel): 6:9-15
IV. The Requirements for and Glory of Full Restoration: 7–8

The series of visions in Zechariah 1–8 contains the major teaching of this prophet. Although scholars are not agreed as to the precise interpretation of each of the visions, it is generally understood that the visions portray a series of events which were necessary for the restoration of the people in the land.

Several of the visions deserve more specific comment. The first observation concerns the scene and characters in the fourth vision, in which the high priest, clothed in filthy garments, was standing before Yahweh. These garments obviously symbolized the sins and uncleanness of the people. After God assured the priest (whose name was Joshua) that the iniquity of the people had been forgiven, the priest was given "rich apparel" and a "clean turban." The teaching of Zechariah at this point is quite similar to that in the famous new covenant passage of Jeremiah in which the prerequisite for a restored community was God's forgiveness of the people.

One very interesting feature contained in this vision is the figure of Satan, the "Accuser." This is probably the first reference in the entire collection of Old Testament writings (arranged chronologically) where Satan has been encountered. His identity here is primarily one relating to function rather than being, for he is depicted here (as elsewhere in the Old Testament) as a member of the court of Yahweh whose duty it was to move about the earth and report the sins of the people to God. The idea of Satan as leader of the demonic forces of cosmic evil and as the epitome of all that is evil did not emerge until the intertestamental period (after 150 B.C.) and was brought about by the influence of apocalyptic thought patterns.

Another major item involves the fifth vision (chapter 4) which rather plainly depicts Zerubbabel as the primary character in the restoration of the new community to new heights of glory. What really happened next is not known, but by the conclusion of the vision sequence Zerubbabel's name has disappeared from the account. Some scholars believe that the caution to this political leader in 4:6 may hold a clue as to what happened. The text reads: "This is the word of the LORD to Zerubbabel: Not by might, nor by power, but by my Spirit says the LORD of hosts." Could this be a reference to an ill-advised attempt by the new community to throw off the authority of the Persians? Certainty cannot be assured, but such an attempt would explain the sudden and complete disappearance of Zerubbabel.

One final comment should be made about 6:9-15. Most scholars believe that this passage originally referred to the coronation of Zerubbabel as the leader of the community, especially since the terminology was more appropriate for a political leader than for a priest (whose presence is now included in the account). The term used here, "the Branch," had been a designation for the political Davidic messiah for some time (Isaiah 11:1; Jeremiah 23:5). Since Zerubbabel disappeared suddenly and Judah was left without any political figure, the emphasis shifted to the importance of the priest alone as *the* leader of the new community.

Zechariah believed that God would cause this people to prosper, Jerusalem would be populated, and the nation would become a nation of significance. He was indeed correct, but the process to accomplish those goals was more lengthy and tedious than he had envisioned or the people wanted (8:1-8). It took about another century for Jerusalem to be rebuilt and repopulated (under the work of Nehemiah) and over three hundred years for the nation to be a strong political entity again.

This prophet, while he truly believed that God would restore the people in Jerusalem and raise them to a place of political respectability, was also a realist. He understood that change often takes longer than overzealous persons are willing to wait.

When such a situation arises it is almost always the zealot who suffers. Trusting in God and relying on his Spirit is more important than rash, ill-conceived, and destructive actions. Even today many persons have not learned that lesson.

ISAIAH 56–66

Having studied the oracles and teachings of Isaiah 1–39 and those included in 40–55, the careful reader finds that the historical setting for the material found in chapters 56–66 differs from that of the other two. Here the covenant people are no longer in Babylonian exile but have returned to Judah and are struggling in their attempt to resettle in the land and become a new nation. The oracles in 56–66 seem to be an attempt to apply the message of Deutero-Isaiah in a new setting. It is most probable that these teachings originated with the group which was preserving and transmitting the teachings of eighth-century Isaiah and Deutero-Isaiah. This would explain the reason why these oracles were included within the prophetic scroll of Isaiah.

One of the major critical problems related to these chapters concerns whether all these oracles originated from the same person or from several persons over the course of a longer time. Scholars are not totally unanimous in their opinion here, but most believe that the materials in 56–66 did come from numerous persons speaking over a long period of time. One finds that some teachings look forward to the building of the temple and some look back at the completed temple and wrestle with the problems of proper worship. Most scholars, therefore, date the oracles incorporated into these chapters from about 520 to 450 B.C.

Great diversity in the teachings can be ascertained by a careful examination of the material. There is the typical postexilic hope that God will restore the community to a position of independence and importance. There are also teachings which remind one of the fiery blasts of the preexilic prophets proclaiming judgment on an evil people. Some of these "zingers" were directed toward certain leaders who were selfish and unscrupulous (56:9-12). Others were aimed at religious leaders who wished to impose only their interpretations upon the community and who emphasized cultic purity without accompanying moral purity (chapter 58). Still others were directed at people in general who refused to act justly in their dealings with society (chapter 59). The oracles included in "Trito-Isaiah," as this collection is sometimes called, did not excuse the people for their sins simply because they were experiencing difficult times.

Study Outline for the Book of Isaiah 56–66

I. The Centrality of the Temple in the New Community: 56:1-8
II. Alternating Oracles of Judgment, Threat, Hope: 56:9–66:24

The entire collection is introduced with a description of the requirements for admission into and participation in the new community of God's people (56:1-8). This is a beautiful passage emphasizing the importance of keeping God's law, of "keeping justice and doing righteousness." It is interesting to note also that this oracle is "inclusive," even foreigners and eunuchs were welcome as participants in the group (before this time "blemished" persons were not considered members of the holy community). The requirements for their participation were the same as for the Judeans: doing righteousness, keeping the law, and most importantly, centering their worship in the Jerusalem temple. "My house shall be called a house of prayer for all peoples" (56:7c).

After this introductory oracle, however, one searches with little success to find a consistent theme or pattern in the remainder of the collection. Several ideas and motifs appear to be presented primarily to challenge the leaders and people to become what the new community of God's people was supposed to be and to describe the marvelous wonders of the new age which still had not arrived but was, nevertheless, expected.

Several passages are worthy of note. Many interpreters believe that the passage in chapters 60–62 formed the nucleus for the entire collection (56–66). Its basic theme is hope for the people that the new age will come. The most interesting portion is found in chapter 61. This passage is important because it is very similar in style and thought to the servant passages of 40–55; in fact, there are some who believe that verses 1-4 should be included with those four poetic songs. These verses are also quite

similar, however, to some of the "call" accounts found in some
of the preexilic prophets (Isaiah 6; Jeremiah 1), the difference
being that the earlier prophets were called to proclaim judgment,
this one to declare "good news."

A second item of note in this portion of the text is the strong
belief that the people of the world would be subservient to the
new community of God's people:

> Aliens shall stand and feed your flocks,
>   foreigners shall be your plowmen and vinedressers; . . .
>   —61:5

This is an interesting turn because already there had been an
oracle which appeared to invite all persons to become a part of
this new community. The divergent points of view incorporated
into this prophetic collection may well represent a real difference
of opinion among the people of the struggling community with
regard to their relationship with the outside world. Some believed very strongly that keeping "pure" necessitated staying
away from outsiders; they argued that if the community was to
preserve its identity and traditions, it would be forced to guard
in every way possible against any deviation or alteration others
might bring. Another group felt that the most appropriate way
to preserve identity and traditions was to invite all who would
to participate in the activities and beliefs of this group. After all,
was this not the very reason for the existence of the nation as
God's special people (Genesis 12:3)? While both viewpoints are
represented in Isaiah 56–66, the more exclusivistic is dominant
as in most of the postexilic prophetic teaching.

A second passage which causes some degree of ambiguity
among interpreters is found in chapter 66. Here is a passage
which appears to have been opposed to the building of the
temple. This negativity is puzzling since most of the remainder
of the teachings speak quite positively about the temple and its
central place among the restored people. Several scholars have
suggested that this passage did not refer to the Jerusalem temple,
but it was addressed to the people in the area of the old Northern
Kingdom (now known as Samaritans). When the Judeans first
returned from Babylonia, these people to the north offered assistance. This offer of help was, however, very ungraciously
rejected, and a bitter relationship began to develop between

these two groups. The feelings became so aggravated that the Samaritans finally decided to build for themselves a rival temple on Mount Gerizim. It is possible that this oracle was directed against the temple to the north, not the temple in Jerusalem.

It is more likely, however, that this passage *was* directed toward the people in Judah. It is not certain that the Samaritan temple was even built during this historical period. The most likely explanation is that this oracle was directed as a warning against those who may have been placing too much trust in the fact that the temple was finally built and, consequently, God was bound to bless the people no matter what they did or said with regard to religious matters. The temple could not be a panacea to cure all the problems and worries the people were experiencing.

The collection concludes with a positive outlook: God would bless these people. The purpose of the blessing was not to insure that these people would be rewarded as much as it was to insure that God's purposes and laws would be accomplished and made known to many peoples.

> For as the new heavens and the new earth
>   which I will make
> shall remain before me, says the LORD;
>   so shall your descendants and your name remain.
> From new moon to new moon,
>   and from sabbath to sabbath,
> all flesh shall come to worship before me,
>   says the LORD.
>
> —66:22-23

In every society there are conflicting points of view as to what should be done to insure the continuation of the society and to improve the quality of its life and the fulfillment of its goals and aspirations. Sometimes these differences of opinion are very sharply debated and held. The collection of oracles in "Trito-Isaiah" reflects some of this debate among the people in the early postexilic community in Judah. In spite of the heated debate, however, there seems to have been a strong understanding that life must revolve around God's commands. The centrality of God in life had to be *the* primary consideration in being the people of God. The ambiguities of the world might sometimes cause uncertainty about the *methods* to be employed to accomplish God's purposes, but the commitment to those purposes had to be strong and unequivocal. One hopes that the day will come when all peoples will worship in the house of God having that commitment to God's justice and righteousness.

OBADIAH

The Book of Obadiah is the shortest of all the Old Testament writings. In content it is quite similar to the prophecy of Nahum, containing an oracle against a foreign nation, here Edom. The people of Edom, south of Judah, were considered to have had family ties with the Israelites somewhere in the distant past. Tradition linked the Edomites with the descendants of Esau, Jacob's brother. The relationship between the two nations, like that between Jacob and Esau, had not always been one of brotherly affection.

Some interpreters date the prophet Obadiah as far back as the eighth century B.C., but it is much more likely that the contents of the proclamation reflect the postexilic times. Obadiah proclaimed Yahweh's judgment on the nation of Edom because it had participated in some type of military conquest of Judah. Many scholars think that this occurred at the time of the destruction of Jerusalem in 586 B.C. when Nebuchadnezzar required some of the smaller nations in the area to participate in the siege. Some of these nations may have volunteered to assist; perhaps Edom was one of those! Other historians think that the most appropriate dating for the event which caused Obadiah to express his anger followed the defeat and destruction of Jerusalem by the Babylonians. The people who were left in the land were especially vulnerable to attack by any group with a will to do so. Perhaps the Edomites took advantage of that time to harass and rob and to confiscate some territory (the Negeb) which had formerly belonged to Judah. Still another theory suggests an attack by the Edomites on the restored community around 485 B.C. in which the Edomites inflicted much damage on the land and even destroyed the new temple. So little is known about the precise history of the postexilic period that any suggestion about dating can be only a hypothesis. It is most likely, however, that a date after 586 B.C. is correct.

Study Outline for the Book of Obadiah

I. Oracle Against Edom: vv. 1-14
II. Oracle About the "Day of Yahweh": vv. 15-21

The major portion of this book simply contains a description of the judgment which would come upon Edom because of its treachery against the people of God. The evils perpetrated by the Edomites are detailed quite specifically.

The last few verses announce the "day of Yahweh," an older concept obviously not yet forgotten. All nations were to stand under the judgment of Yahweh, but Edom was to feel his wrath most harshly. The book concludes with the recurring postexilic hope that the fortunes of the old united monarchy might be restored (vv. 19-21).

This book, as already indicated, is similar in many respects to that of Nahum. Very little can be added to what was suggested there (see pp. 67-69). The teaching is clear: those who violate God's laws and prey upon the helpless stand under judgment.

JONAH

The Book of Jonah is unique within the prophetic literature, for it is a story about a prophet named Jonah—not a collection of oracles. This story has been a source of some misunderstanding and heated discussion for several generations. The basic reason for this situation is the fact that most persons have not been aware of the literary developments in Israelite history, especially in the postexilic period. As has been mentioned earlier, there was a movement in Israel known as the wisdom movement. It received a major endorsement under the kingship of Solomon, famous for his wisdom. This movement developed certain styles of teaching usually using *comparison* type stories or sayings called *mashal* in Hebrew. These stories included such types as fables, allegories, parables, short pithy sayings, or short stories which usually made points by the comparisons that could be drawn between the story and the readers or hearers. Obviously these stories did not need to be historically true, as some suggest, in order to present the intended lessons. This type of wisdom

flowered in the postexilic community; and most reputable scholars are agreed that the account of Jonah is essentially a "wisdom"
type story, told to draw a comparison between the story and
the intended audience.

The story is set in preexilic times when Assyria was the dominant nation in that area. Even though there is a prophet named
Jonah mentioned in 2 Kings 14:25, very little is known of him.
Some have attempted to identify that Jonah with the Jonah of
the book, but that is unlikely. The book was most probably
written in the postexilic times because the language and style
of writing reflect postexilic Hebrew literary usage, not that of
preexilic days. There are certain indications in the text itself that
at the time of the writing Nineveh was a city of the past; for
Nineveh never existed exactly as it is described in Jonah. The
setting for such a story within the development of the Hebrew
religion is much more appropriate in the postexilic period, as
well.

Study Outline for the Book of Jonah

  I. Jonah Called to Preach to Nineveh: 1:1-16
 II. Jonah Swallowed by the Fish: 1:17–2:9
III. Jonah Preaches to Nineveh: 2:10–3:10
 IV. Jonah's Response to Nineveh's Repentance: 4:1-
     11

The story of Jonah moves quickly from one episode to another.
The prophet was called to preach to Nineveh, the city of the
hated Assyrians. Instead of obeying God's call, Jonah took passage on a ship bound for Tarshish (in Spain), as far in the
opposite direction as he could go. God then caused a great storm
to endanger the boat. By lot Jonah was discovered to be the one
responsible for the problem. He told the pagan sailors to throw
him overboard, but they tried as best they could to save Jonah's
life. When it became obvious that the cause was lost, Jonah was
thrown overboard.

God had prepared a special fish to swallow Jonah. Whether
this fish was intended to be understood literally or symbolically
has been debated for many generations. Because this is a story,
specifically a comparison-type story, there is every likelihood

that the fish is symbolic, probably representing the exile of the people in Babylon. (The meaning of the story is the same no matter which theory one chooses.) Jonah cried out in distress for God to deliver him, and the fish vomited Jonah onto the dry land. (Jonah was obviously indigestible and unpalatable!) God then commanded him again to go preach to Nineveh.

Jonah's preaching, surprisingly enough, caused these pagan people to repent. Rather than rejoicing at such marvelous success, Jonah became very angry. The truth became known. He had not run away because he was afraid of failure, or ridicule, or even death. Jonah had fled because he did not want the people of Nineveh to have the opportunity to repent. "That is why I made haste to flee to Tarshish; for I know that you are a gracious God, merciful, slow to anger, running over in covenant loyalty and that you change your mind about doing evil" (4:2b, paraphrase). The point is clear enough.

Jonah remained outside the city in the hope that God would yet destroy it. A plant then grew up over Jonah, but a worm attacked it and it withered (both plant and worm were "appointed" by Yahweh). Jonah became even more angry. God asked him if his anger were justified, and Jonah argued strongly that it was. The book then abruptly ends with the dramatic words of God: "You pity the plant, for which you did not labor, nor did you make it grow, which came into being in a night, and perished in a night. And should not I pity Nineveh, that great city, in which there are more than a hundred and twenty thousand persons who do not know their right hand from their left, and also much cattle?" (4:10-11).

Jonah's narrow vision, selfish nature, and bitterness are clearly highlighted in this story. One recalls that the postexilic community had a growing tendency to become more narrow and exclusivisitic. Some of this thinking was caused by the appropriate desire that the fragile community be preserved and survive as a unique entity, but some thinking had gone far beyond survival. There must have been some who questioned the extreme views held by those who advocated radical separateness from the other peoples of the world. How, indeed, could God's people be a light to the nations and fulfill their purpose of election if they excluded themselves from the world? Another question also seems to be implicit: why such an emphasis on being exclusivistic? Was it really for purposes of survival, or was the motivation something less honorable? Did these people really want to share God's blessing with others?

It appears, then, that the story of Jonah definitely fits into the historical period of the postexilic community. The comparisons made between the story and the people are quite clear. They had rejected Yahweh's elective call to make him known to the world and had experienced a traumatic event which should have caused them to repent. However, in spite of all this, they had not really learned what was required in having been selected to such a responsible task. The Book of Jonah called them back with this story—a story which was filled with not-so-subtle challenges.

As with most "wisdom-" type stories, the hearers or readers are challenged to draw comparisons between themselves and those around them, not only personally but situationally. The message of Jonah and its challenges are just as fitting in certain modern settings as the book was when first written. Who can fail to see the integrity of the pagan sailors risking their own lives to save the life of Jonah? Or the callousness of Jonah who did not want the people of Nineveh to experience God's mercy and forgiveness? We do not require a learned intellectual to make modern comparisons for us; that is one of the beauties of wisdom stories. God cares for all people—even for their animals (4:11)!

MALACHI

The prophetic teachings included in the Book of Malachi are probably to be dated in the time period from the rebuilding of the temple (ca. 515 B.C.) to the reform movements of Nehemiah and Ezra (ca. 450 B.C.). The historical references fit this era more closely than any other. Even though the teachings appear to be the product of one person, this individual's name is unknown. The name which has become attached to these sayings is, of course, Malachi, but that name is derived from a descriptive title. In the Hebrew text the term means "my messenger" and is found in 1:1 and 3:1. This was not considered a proper name at first; in the Greek translation of the Hebrew Old Testament (made around 300–100 B.C.) this term is rendered simply as "my messenger," not as a proper name. Later development led to the idea that Malachi was the name of this prophet, and he has been known by that designation for many centuries now.

There is a critical problem of some consequence associated with this book and the concluding chapters of Zechariah, 9–14. The material in Zechariah 1–8 (see discussion on pp. 100-103) appears to be a self-contained unit, orginating from the period of the rebuilding of the temple (520–515 B.C.). After that collection, there are three units of prophetic material of almost equal length each beginning with the word, "oracle." Two of these three came to be attached to the Book of Zechariah and the other came to be known as Malachi. None of these three, however, is dated or has a person specifically named as the prophet who delivered the teachings. Most scholars, therefore, believe that these three collections of prophetic teachings were placed at the conclusion of the much larger work which came to be known among the Jewish people as the "Book of the Twelve." These teachings were obviously understood to be of significance and value and appropriate for the conclusion of the entire prophetic collection. Whether the separation of the first two from the third of these collections (and the inclusion of those first two with Zechariah 1–8) was made by the original editors or by some later persons working on the text is not known. Whatever happened occurred very early because the collection was known rather early as the Book of the Twelve.

The material in Malachi was obviously understood as an appropriate conclusion to the larger collection. The postexilic community, in which the collection was made, was still looking forward to a new age which had not materialized. These prophetic teachings definitely anticipate the establishment of such an era, which would come if the people were ceremonially and morally prepared for it. A time of judgment would occur, as would a new appearance of the prophetic spirit. This idea is found in the reference to Elijah (4:5-6), who was understood to be the embodiment of the prophetic movement. The reference to the return of Elijah should not be taken literally; such terminology was quite usual for those times, epitomizing an entire movement in one personality. Elijah's original ministry had involved calling the people back to the worship of Yahweh, challenging them to be faithful. The teachings in this collection of sayings are, therefore, a most fitting summary of the prophetic movement and a looking forward to a new period of even closer relationship with God.

Study Outline for the Book of Malachi
I. Yahweh's Love for His People: 1:1-5
II. Oracle Against the People and Priests: 1:6–2:9
III. Oracle Against Marriage Violations: 2:10-16
IV. God's Sure Judgment on Sin: 2:17–3:5
V. Why Present Troubles Have Come: 3:6-12
VI. The Coming of a New Age: 3:13–4:6

This entire collection is set immediately within the context of the prophet's understanding that God loved the people of Judah. Obviously Edom had recently suffered some sort of devastation which Judah had escaped, and this was viewed as proof of God's commitment to the people. Such gracious action on God's part, however, required greater response and commitment on the part of the people.

Things were apparently not as they should be, especially when religious obligations were involved. The people were accused of offering blemished animals for sacrifice, and the priests accepted them! Yahweh's requirements were not being placed first in their lives. Another matter of serious concern was the fact that Jewish men had been divorcing their wives to marry non-Jewish women. Why the men were doing this is not exactly clear, but many scholars think that the practice arose from the attempt on the part of the men to obtain some type of financial security. They were marrying women primarily from the northern area, probably because these families were well established and could offer economic and political connections.

The prophet indicated clearly that judgment would surely come upon those who violated God's requirements—not only on the pagan peoples of the world but also God's community in Judah. It is interesting that such comments still needed to be made, especially in the light of the harsh judgments experienced in 721 and 586 B.C. Hard times were continuing because the people had not fulfilled the requirements with regard to cultic affairs. There was great apathy on their part concerning the sacrifices, offerings, and the tithe. Failure to observe those requirements reflected an overall lack of concern for the centrality of God and his requirements in their lives, and such an attitude invited trouble.

The people were challenged to do right and warned that God's judgment was certain. Even more pointedly, this prophet told the people that judgment would begin at the house of Yahweh (3:1). The new age, while not yet present, would surely come; the people, therefore, had to be properly prepared. It is interesting to note that the reference to the coming of Elijah, while emphasizing the prophetic challenge to be true worshipers of Yahweh, showed Elijah's primary task as that of restoring the family unit, something that was a matter of great concern at that particular moment.

The teachings of Malachi were quite similar to many others of the postexilic period. The community was struggling and thought that to some extent they could be excused for certain laxity toward religious matters; according to the prophetic voices, they could not. Adherence to God's requirements was neither optional nor conditional. Hard times were no excuse for failure to complete Yahweh's commands.

There is in this collection of teachings, however, an unmistakable promise of hope. This hope was not a result of wishful thinking on the part of the prophet but centered in his understanding of God. Yahweh loved the people and wanted to do good for them; yet these divine wishes were not to be considered absolute and unconditional. Human beings have always wanted to interpret God's promises in that way, with no strings attached. The prophets understood that even in religious matters there was no such thing as a "free lunch." They never believed that God's grace could be earned or deserved or demanded; but, apart from a positive response from those to whom the grace was offered, that grace could not and would not be effective. How difficult it seems to be for the human race to learn this clear and specific teaching of the prophets!

JOEL

Dating the prophet Joel is the major problem in dealing with this book. Some have argued that Joel was the earliest of the prophets, locating him in the ninth century B.C.; others think that he must have been the latest, dating the setting in the second century B.C. There are, of course, many conjectures in between. The book seems to reflect a postexilic historical setting since there is a reference to the exile of Judah (3:1-3), several references to the reconstructed temple (1:9, 14, 16; 2:17; 3:18), and perhaps an allusion to the rebuilt walls (2:7, 9).

The major question revolves around exactly where in the postexilic period these oracles fit. The historical setting seems to reflect a period of difficult times for the community probably associated with some form of military activity in or near Judah. The most likely time would have been during, or shortly after, the military conquests of Alexander the Great in this area and the wars fought by Alexander's successors after his early and unexpected death in 323 B.C. It is most probable that the prophecy of Joel originated during this period of history, since there is a reference to the "Greeks" in 3:6.

Several interesting theories have been suggested regarding the composition of the book. One of the most interesting presents the idea that Joel is composed of two separate collections, one (chapters 1–2) originating in preexilic times and the second (chapters 3–4, the Hebrew text being divided into four chapters) originating in the postexilic era. It is quite possible that there may have been early materials incorporated into the text of this prophetic message, but a close examination does not really lend support to such a theory. Its date is almost assuredly postexilic.

Study Outline for the Book of Joel

I. Vision of Devastation: 1:1–2:11
II. Call to Repentance: 2:12-17
III. God's Response: 2:18-32
IV. Judgment of Judah's Enemies 3:1-21

There is a rather orderly and logical progression in the presentation of the material in this book. The first section depicts a scene of devastation brought about by locusts and drought. One of the major interpretative discussions revolves around the identity of the "locusts." Many scholars understand this as a literal plague of locusts which stripped the land—a dreaded and terrible occurrence for any people in those days (and even today). The locust plague and subsequent drought were understood as a judgment sent by God. Other interpreters understand the "locusts" as an invading army, since this symbol was used in those days for a military invasion. Whether one understands this figure as a natural catastrophe or as a military conquest, the meaning is the same. Judgment had come because of the sin of the people. It is also interesting to note that the destruction was not confined to Judah but seemed to have affected a large number of nations in that area of the world. In Joel the old term, "day of Yahweh," seemed to indicate a judgment on many nations, which would precede the coming of the new age for God's people.

The call to repentance then was sounded. "Rend your hearts and not your garments" (2:13a). If the people truly repented, God would forgive them, and indeed bring in the new age. One of the most famous of all Joel's oracles depicted this "new age" idea (2:24-29), especially the latter verses:

> And it shall come to pass afterward,
>   that I will pour out my spirit on all flesh;
> your sons and your daughters shall prophesy,
>   your old men shall dream dreams,
>   and your young men shall see visions.
> Even upon the menservants and maidservants
>   in those days, I will pour out my spirit.
> —2:28-29

One of the most fascinating twists in any of the prophetic literature is found in Joel. Since there was so much destruction in the area, the prophet obviously felt that the people had to defend themselves (as best they could) from the invaders. He urged:

> "Beat your plowshares into swords,
>   and your pruning hooks into spears. . . ."
> —3:10

Joel believed that the new age would come soon, brought about because Yahweh would defend his people and judge their enemies. This prophet was able to see in the course of human history (or perhaps natural events) the hand of God seeking to bring his purposes to completion. Human ambition and struggle for power will ultimately come to nought since these are not in accordance with God's will. Again one notes that human participation in the ongoing course of history is exceedingly important, and that certain situations sometimes call for differing modes of action. One hopes always to be able to "beat swords into plowshares," but there may be times when the people of God must act on their own behalf and in their own defense. Stupidity is not a corollary of faith, nor should it be.

ZECHARIAH 9–14

These chapters of Zechariah (9–14) have already been mentioned in relation to the Book of Malachi. They comprise two of the three collections of oracles placed at the conclusion of the Book of the Twelve, being divided into chapters 9–11 and 12–14. Each section should be examined individually so that one can ascertain what relation, if any, it has with the prophet Zechariah and/ or to the other section.

The question of authorship simply cannot be resolved. Who the prophet or prophets were whose sayings were collected in these chapters cannot be determined. There are practically no clues. Some have suggested that there are enough similarities between the scroll of Isaiah and the Book of Zechariah to argue for a Zechariah "school" from which emerged these prophetic sayings. It is, therefore, not unusual to read in some scholars about a Deutero- and Trito-Zechariah. Other interpreters argue that this material came from several different sources and was not originally connected with any "school." Not enough evidence is available to make a statement with any degree of specificity.

Dating the material is another problem with varying theories. Suggestions have ranged from the preexilic period to the Maccabean era (beginning about 167 B.C.). Some scholars think that chapters 9–11 are preexilic, while 12–14 are postexilic. Most, however, date all these materials from the postexilic period. The linguistic evidence as well as historical references point to that time. The siege of Tyre by Alexander (332 B.C.) may well have been the basis for the description in 9:1-8, and the literary style of 12–14 reflects apocalyptic thought patterns which probably only developed in the late third century B.C.

Although there are no clear solutions to the problems attached to Zechariah 9–14, it is most likely that the collections were composed of oracles from different prophets during the later postexilic period. Various themes run through the collections, and it is difficult to outline them with any degree of consistency. Both collections, however, look forward to a new age in which Jerusalem would be the center for a community of nations.

Study Outline for the Book of Zechariah 9–14

I. Various Oracles of Judgment, Challenge, and Hope: 9–11

II. God's People Delivered, the New Age Established: 12–14

The first section begins with a description of judgment on the nations surrounding Judah. This would then lead to a period of peace, something the Jewish people in the time of Alexander and his successors would welcome. The period of peace was to be inaugurated by the figure of a triumphant king riding into Jerusalem upon an ass (9:9). The oracle continues with a discussion of the greatness of Yahweh, especially as he controlled history and nature, as well as descriptions of Yahweh's anger against leaders who did not lead and who cared nothing for the people entrusted to their keeping. Obviously at that period the leaders of the community were unscrupulous, and there is some evidence that the people may have gotten what they deserved (11:4-6).

In the second collection there is a stern warning to the community to cleanse itself of idolatry and sin. The implication seems to have been that the new age had not yet come because the people had not yet prepared themselves to receive it. There was hope, however, because the new age could still come, and the text gives a moving and sometimes shocking description of the glory and greatness of the new age (chapter 14). There was a note of universalism in this portrait (all nations could become members of God's community), but there was no question as to which people would have the central place and exercise authority on behalf of God. Jerusalem would become the center of the world in the new age.

CHAPTER 4

Conclusion

The prophetic movement spanned several centuries. Its existence was closely tied to the political movement connected with the establishment of the monarchy and the nation. The prophets continued to participate in the nation's destiny, however, for some time into the postexilic period, even though the nation as a political entity had not been reestablished. The postexilic hope for the recreation of the nation to its former status was constantly thwarted by the grim realities of history, but these religious personalities continued to hope for a new age and constantly challenged the people to live up to their covenant obligation, even interpreting the delay in the coming of the new age as a result of the sins of the people and their leaders.

Many other religious developments were taking place during the postexilic period, however, which reflected the continuing struggle of the community to understand God's will and the community's own past, present, and future. The rise of new movements which spoke to the needs of the people hastened the demise of the prophetic movement *per se*. The teachings of the prophets were obviously revered, preserved, transmitted, and finally placed in written form so that their revelations might speak to new generations within the community of God's people.

Perhaps one final comment should be made concerning the prophets and their teachings because so many misinterpretations have been perpetuated about them. The prophets were primarily proclaimers of God's message to the people in certain concrete historical settings, and whatever predicting they did was limited to their immediate future and specifically related to the peoples of Israel and Judah in that precise moment of history.

For example, the predictions of restoration of the people of Judah into the land of Judah were directed toward the exiles in Babylonia. Those predictions materialized as the prophets had said. Further, the anticipation of a new age in which the community in Judah would enjoy political freedom again was addressed to the people living in the postexilic era. Though that dream did not materialize immediately, the fault, according to the prophets, lay in the lack of dedication on the part of the people and the incompetence and immorality of the leaders. Eventually, however, the time came when the nation became independent and was ruled over by a priest-king (141–63 B.C), thus fulfilling the hope of the postexilic prophets.

Many persons are misled by thinking that these ancient prophets were predicting modern historical events, nations, and people. They were not! To use such interpretations to support modern ideologies is to misuse and misunderstand the texts in their plain meanings. If there are modern situations which are analogous to the situations of those times, the principles and truths which were relevant then will be relevant now. These principles can be applied because they are God's revealed truths.

The messages of the prophets cannot, however, be made to carry meanings that they obviously did not have for the prophets and people at the time when they were originally delivered. The method of interpretation which attempts to find predictions of present or future events in the prophetic writings, while very popular in some circles and among some very sincere people, does violence to the biblical word. What is needed in the study of the prophetic messages is a dedication to understanding what the prophetic books really say rather than finding in them support for pet theories and popular causes about which the writers of these books knew nothing.

The messages of the prophets are still relevant because the religious truths they proclaimed are authoritative for all time. The modern interpreter must be very careful, however, to find the proper and analogous setting in which to apply the teaching. Our hope should be that modern generations will hear the prophets and take their teachings more seriously than the people to whom they originally spoke. For truly these prophets were, and still are, the voices of God.

FOR FURTHER STUDY

GENERAL INTRODUCTION

Roland E. Clements, *Prophecy and Tradition.* Atlanta: John Knox Press, 1975.

Norman K. Gottwald, *All the Kingdoms of the Earth.* New York: Harper & Row, Publishers, Inc., 1964.

Abraham J. Heschel, *The Prophets of Israel.* New York: Harper & Row, Publishers, Inc., 1962.

Johannes Lindblom, *Prophecy in Ancient Israel.* Philadelphia: Fortress Press, 1962. *Note: A classic, but heavy reading.*

Harry Mowvley, *Reading the Old Testament Prophets Today.* Atlanta: John Knox Press, 1979.

Gerhard von Rad, *The Message of the Prophets.* Trans. D. M. G. Stalker. London: SCM Press, 1968.

Claus Westermann, *Basic Forms of Prophetic Speech.* Trans. H. C. White. Philadelphia: The Westminster Press, 1967.

Robert R. Wilson, *Prophecy and Society in Ancient Israel.* Philadelphia: Fortress Press, 1980.

INDIVIDUAL WORKS

Amos

James L. Mays, *Amos: A Commentary.* Philadelphia: The Westminster Press, 1969.

Henry McKeating, *Amos, Hosea, and Micah.* New York: Cambridge University Press, 1971.

James M. Ward, *Amos and Isaiah: Prophets of the Word of God.* Nashville: Abingdon Press, 1969.

Hosea

James L. Mays, *Hosea: A Commentary.* Philadelphia: The Westminster Press, 1969.

James M. Ward, *Hosea: A Theological Commentary.* New York: Harper & Row, Publishers, Inc., 1966.

Isaiah 1–39

William L. Holladay, *Isaiah: Scroll of a Prophetic Heritage.* Grand Rapids, Mich.: Wm. B. Eerdmans Publishing Co., 1978.

Otto Kaiser, Isaiah 1–12. Trans. R. A. Wilson. Philadelphia: The Westminster Press, 1972.

_____, *Isaiah 13–39.* Trans. R. A. Wilson. Philadelphia: The Westminster Press, 1973.

Jeremiah

John Bright, ed., *Jeremiah.* Garden City, N. Y.: Doubleday & Co., Inc., n.d.

James M. Efird, *Jeremiah: Prophet Under Siege.* Valley Forge: Judson Press, 1979.

E. W. Nicholson, *The Book of the Prophet Jeremiah: Chapters 1-25.* New York: Cambridge University Press, 1973.

_____, *The Book of the Prophet Jeremiah: Chapters 28-52.* New York: Cambridge University Press, 1975.

Ezekiel

Walther Eichrodt, *Ezekiel.* Trans. Cosslett Quin. Philadelphia: The Westminster Press, 1970.

James L. Mays, *Ezekiel, Second Isaiah.* Philadelphia: Fortress Press, 1978.

J. W. Wevers, *Ezekiel.* London: Thomas Nelson & Sons, 1969.

Isaiah 40–55, 56–66

John L. McKenzie, *Second Isaiah*. Anchor Bible Series, vol. 20. Garden City, N.Y.: Doubleday & Co., Inc., 1968.

Christopher R. North, *Isaiah 40-55*. New York: Macmillan, Inc., n.d.

—————, *The Suffering Servant in Deutero-Isaiah*, 2nd ed. New York: Oxford University Press, 1956.

James D. Smart, *History and Theology in Second Isaiah: A Commentary on Isaiah 35, 40-66*. Philadelphia: The Westminster Press, 1965.

Claus Westermann, *Isaiah 40-66: A Commentary*. Trans. D. M. G. Stalker. Philadelphia: The Westminster Press, 1969.

R. N. Whybray, ed., *Isaiah 40-66*. London: Oliphants; Greenwood, S. C.: Attic Press, 1975.

Books on Others of the Twelve Prophets

T. E. Fretheim, *The Message of Jonah*. Minneapolis, Minn.: Augsburg Publishing House, 1976.

Donald E. Gowan, *The Triumph of Faith in Habakkuk*. Atlanta: John Knox Press, 1976.

Rex Mason, *The Books of Haggai, Zechariah, and Malachi*. New York: Cambridge University Press, 1977.

James L. Mays, *Micah: A Commentary*. Philadelphia: The Westminster Press, 1976.

John D. W. Watts, *The Books of Joel, Obadiah, Jonah, Nahum, Habakkuk, and Zephaniah*. New York: Cambridge University Press, 1975.